sabrina's
juicy little book of
citrus

First published 2012 by
FREMANTLE PRESS
25 Quarry Street, Fremantle 6160
(PO Box 158, North Fremantle 6159)
Western Australia
www.fremantlepress.com.au

Reprinted 2015, 2018.

Editor Naama Amram
Designer Tracey Gibbs
Cover photo and inside photo by Tracey Gibbs
Printed by Everbest Printing Company, China

National Library of Australia Cataloguing-in-Publication entry
Author: Hahn, Sabrina.
Title: Sabrina's juicy little book of citrus / Sabrina Hahn.
ISBN: 9781921888984 (pbk.)
Notes: Includes index.
Subjects: Citrus.
Dewey Number: 634.304

Fremantle Press is supported by the State Government
through the Department of Culture and the Arts.

Government of **Western Australia**
Department of **Culture and the Arts**

sabrina's
juicy little book of
citrus

Sabrina Hahn

 **FREMANTLE PRESS**

Contents

Introduction

There is a trend for gardening books on fruit growing to be heavy on photos and light on information. Welcome to this little book which is solid information and no photos. Coming from a long line of gardeners, I know that good information makes the difference between persevering and giving up. It also arms you with the confidence to try something you may have had no experience with.

This book is for both experienced and novice gardeners. It aims to enable you to get the most out of your citrus trees and to circumvent the ongoing barrage of lemon tree questions on my gardening talkback radio programs. It covers just about everything you need to know to have success – the good, the bad and the ugly. The content of this little book is 90 per cent optimistic with just a tinge of 'What the hell is that?' to keep the experienced gardeners honest.

If there were no citrus in the world, I believe there would be no gardening talkback programs going to air. In the twenty years I have been doing talkback radio, there has never been a program where citrus tree questions didn't pop up. So frequently in fact that producers screen the calls and cap them at three per program.

The reason citrus questions are so prominent is because just about every home has some sort of citrus. Lemon trees would be the most popular by far. They produce as much offspring as a fertile rabbit and are easy to grow *once* established. In their younger years, however, all citrus need to be treated with love and attention – the spoilt children of the garden.

Citrus are long-lived trees and compared to other fruit trees are relatively trouble-free. Adding to their princess status, the blossom is overwhelmingly seductive and the bright green foliage is delicious. Citrus will grow in an enormous variety of climates and soil types and nearly all Australians can have a decent crack at growing these rewarding trees in their gardens.

I haven't even mentioned the health benefits of eating citrus straight from the tree. There's more vitamin C in red capsicums and brussels sprouts than in oranges and lemons, but I know which I prefer to pig out on. Having a citrus tree in your garden will bring a few months of frustration in the early years and then years of joy and an avalanche of delicious fruit that have more uses than a Swiss Army Knife.

The citrus family is an enormous one and its members include sweet oranges, grapefruits, pomelos, bitter oranges, kumquats, calamondins, mandarins, tangelos, lemons, limes and citrons. The list of citrus varieties I selected for this book may seem long, but it's much longer for those I left out. Whatever your citrus, the general care is about the same for all.

How citrus travelled the earth

Citrus has a very long and interesting history. Chinese writings from 500 BC mention the fruit and flower of the citron, the oldest known citrus species. It is thought that modern citrus originated in southern China. The spread of citrus is definitely connected with the trade routes of ancient China. The ability to propagate citrus from seeds and buds ensured its travel ticket to new worlds.

The Chinese were great travellers and sailed the southern seas long before the English, Dutch and French. Their ships carried potted citrus for the prevention of scurvy, and seeds were planted in areas where colonies were established.

The writings of the Persians, ancient Greeks, Egyptians and Hebrews all make mention of the citron species. When Alexander the Great conquered parts of Asia his armies brought back the citron, which then entered the Roman Empire. The Romans' interest in horticulture and food plants enabled them to grow and import lemons and oranges into Italy. By the height of the Roman Empire I should imagine many cultivars had been developed.

Every empire eventually falls, and the weakened Roman state succumbed to the rise of Islamic power. The Arabs were great traders and seafarers and took the cultivation of citrus into Spain and Africa. It wasn't until the era of the Crusades that oranges, lemons, citrons and limes entered the European world, around the eleventh century. It must be remembered most of the citrus was bitter – the modern sweet orange was a long way off yet.

In Europe of course lemons and oranges had a very illustrious and glamorous status. The grand houses and palaces in Italy, France, Spain and Portugal had hothouses specifically designed to overwinter the trees safely. They were called orangeries or limonaias. Henry IV of France had an elaborate orangery that started the trend which reached epic proportions during the seventeenth and eighteenth centuries. Once Louis XIV included an orangery in Versailles it became a must-have addition to the snootiest and wealthiest families in France.

The early orangeries were really just warmed rooms with very little light. Once glazed windows were available, that revolutionised the design. Elaborate greenhouses started appearing as exotic plants from the new worlds became desired in Europe. The greenhouses were heated with coal stoves and huge pots were wheeled in and out to suit the seasons.

Having seen the size of some of the pots in the privately owned gardens in Italy, Spain and France, I really feel for the gardeners who performed the task of moving them. I have no doubt the odd terracotta pot was dropped as pulleys and levers and gardeners all grunted their way around the pathways and stairs. Citrus trees were highly prized and fed on a diet of milk and honey for the first few weeks of spring to encourage new root development. Special potters were commissioned and you will still find their insignia on some of the oldest pots in the historic gardens of Europe.

Citrus arrived in Australia with the First Fleet in 1788 and has been a popular homegrown fruit ever since.

Captain Phillip wisely picked up a few trees in Rio de Janeiro on his long journey to Australia. The first fruiting trees to arrive must have made an interesting study for those early botanists and nurserymen. With little knowledge of our seasons and the many insects we have here, it was probably a frustrating learning experience.

Kangaroos, parrots, possums, plagues of locusts, grasshoppers, droughts and frosts would have had a huge toll on initial plantings. Added to that would be the pests and diseases that were brought over with the first plants. Amazingly, against all odds, by 1910 there were 270,000 citrus trees recorded in Australia.

The first place to grow citrus on a commercial scale was Parramatta in New South Wales. The climate and soil type were ideal for oranges and I still remember my grandmother asking for Parramatta oranges 'because they were the sweetest'.

Now the citrus industry in Australia is one of the largest horticultural industries, worth around $540 million domestically, plus fresh exports worth $190 million. We have around 2,000 commercial growers across Australia, in every state. We have come a long way.

There has been a lot of research to develop rootstocks that enable gardeners to grow citrus in just about every region in Australia. Rootstocks are very important to the success of your tree and there are now many different species available for lemons, oranges and limes.

The majority of citrus we buy is grafted on particular rootstock that nurseries choose to suit local climate and soil type. Nearly all citrus types are self-pollinated, which can be detrimental if you plant different varieties together that do cross. Your seedless mandarin may end up seeded if planted too close to a seeded tree.

More Facts

Citrus plants will flower on and off all year round if it is warm and moist. They will produce so many flowers that only 9 per cent will actually develop into fruit. The fruit will hang on for months before ripening. It is normal to see flowers developing when a crop is still on the tree.

All citrus flowers have both the male and female parts necessary to be self-fertile. For this reason you only need to plant one tree to get fruit. Insects still play an important role in citrus reproduction: they transfer the pollen from the male part of the flowers to the female part.

Propagation and care

Propagation

Citrus can be propagated by seed, cuttings, aerial layering, or budding and grafting onto selected rootstocks. Most of our citrus today is grown by grafting budstock onto a rootstock seedling. Few people grow citrus from seed because of its high genetic variability, but basically that's how citrus conquered the world. You couldn't get a better container to carry seeds on long journeys than the fruit they're in.

Growing from seed

The most important factor is to use a fresh seed. Once you have picked the fruit from a tree, wash the seeds and plant them in a seed raising mix in a warm spot out of the sun. Choose fat seeds; you can float them in water – the seeds that float will not have an embryo and should be discarded. Each seed should be planted at a depth equal to twice its height.

Use a fine mist to water the seed trays. Germination will occur within 3 weeks. Young seedlings may be pricked out 2 weeks after germination. Interestingly, a citrus seed can produce more than one plant per seed – sometimes up to four – and they will be identical to the parent plant. These are called nucellar embryos. Some seeds may be the result of cross-pollination and will have

Pricking out seedlings

the diversity of the two parents. Citron and pomelo are monoembryonic, meaning each individual seed has only one embryo.

If it's all too much to think about the polyembryonic and monoembryonic state of a seed, these are fabulous words to use in a sentence at boring parties. You will find most people will either leave you alone or stop talking.

There are risks to growing your citrus from seed and one of them has to do with age: it can take anything from six to thirty years before you see any fruit. If you are young enough that this doesn't bother you, give it a go – you could discover a new variety. The downside is that many seedling trees are full of thorns and susceptible to diseases.

Growing from cuttings

Citrus can be grown from leaf bud, semi-hardwood and softwood cuttings. Depending on the type of citrus, you can wait from 4 months to a year before the cutting has good root development.

Let's go for the easiest one first for the keen novice gardener.

Leaf bud cuttings

These are easy to play with. It's best to have everything ready and prepared before you take the cuttings so they don't dry out. You will need:

- Seed trays
- Hormone gel for softwood cuttings
- Seed raising mix
- Clean sterilised secateurs (wipe the blades with methylated spirits)
- A spray bottle filled with water

Take several cuttings along a branch. Each cutting should have a bud (it's where the leaf junction comes from, but remove the leaf) and a piece of stem that is about

6–10 mm long. The stem will need to have a piece above the bud and a piece below the bud. It will look like this (before you've removed the leaf):

Leaf bud cutting

Dip the bottom bit of the stem into the hormone gel (you will know what the bottom bit is because the bud should be facing up) and put upright into the seed raising mix.

Using a spray bottle wet the whole area and cover the seed tray with a lid to prevent loss of moisture. Keep in a warm place out of the sun; allow air in during the day and close it up again at night.

The cuttings should form roots and shoot away in 4 weeks. They will then need to be transplanted into individual pots in a good quality potting mix until they are large enough to pot up again into a larger container.

Semi-hardwood cuttings

You will need:

- A large pot or several pots
- Propagation mix
- Hormone gel for semi-hardwood cuttings
- Wire
- Bubble wrap and tape
- Secateurs
- A spray bottle filled with water

These are the largest cuttings from stems and will need to be 10–30 cm long. These cuttings must be kept warm and moist at all times. You can plant up to 4 cuttings in a large pot.

Again have the pots, wire and bubble wrap all ready before you take the cuttings. Fill the pots up with the propagation mix and water it till it's damp but not soaking. After taking the cuttings, remove the lower two thirds of leaves. You will only have a few leaves left at the top of each cutting.

With a pencil, prepare holes in the propagation mix for the cuttings to slip into.

Scrape a small amount of the bark diagonally off the bottom two centimetres of each cutting and dip this end into the hormone gel.

Slip the cuttings into the holes and push the propagation mix around them to make them stable. Make sure the mix is damp and then mist spray the cuttings.

Create a wire frame by pushing two arched wires into the pot and cover it entirely in bubble wrap, top and sides. Make sure the plastic does not touch the cuttings.

Keep the pot covered until you think it may be drying out. Only use the mist spray to water the cuttings and always cover up the pot again until you see roots developing at its bottom. It may take up to 4 weeks. The cuttings then can be pricked out and potted up into slightly larger pots.

Softwood cuttings

You will need:

- A polystyrene foam box
- Propagation mix
- Hormone gel for softwood cuttings
- Plastic wrap
- Secateurs
- A spray bottle filled with water

These are cuttings taken from new growth and will only be 5–8 cm long. They will be floppy at the top and will need high humidity and moisture to form roots. One of the best things the home gardening enthusiast can use to propagate softwood cuttings is those foam polystyrene boxes that your cold seafood or veggies come in. They are leak-proof, insulated and you can put a plastic wrap cover over them to allow light in while keeping them sealed. You will need to place the box out of direct sunlight but in a warm spot.

Have everything ready before you take the cuttings. Fill the foam box with propagation mix, water it and use a pencil to make little holes for the cuttings.

Take the cuttings from the new soft growth and dip the bottom into the hormone gel. Plant them into the foam box and spray them with water.

Wrap the top of the box completely with plastic wrap and leave all snug and tight for 2 weeks without lifting the wrap. Mist spray once again and rewrap. They should form roots within 2–3 weeks and then can be pricked out and potted up into slightly larger pots.

Budding and grafting

All the trees you purchase from the nursery with the exception of Lots-a-Lemons (it's grown by cuttings) will be a selected variety (the scion) that has been grafted onto a rootstock. The benefit of this is that you will have an identical tree to the one the scion is derived from. This is great because you know what you are getting.

More gardeners should try their hand at grafting – it's a great way to grow your own fruit and bud grafting is the easiest. You can also rework old varieties that you don't want anymore or that have more than one variety on a tree. Grafting for citrus usually takes place in spring or early autumn and budding is done in spring, summer or late summer when the sap is more active.

A bit of terminology that will help you understand what grafting is all about:

Scions (not a planet that Captain Kirk visits) are small pieces of stem that have 1–6 buds, taken from a donor tree. A scion will be identical to the parent plant and once established becomes the major part of the stem system on the new plant. This is your new tree.

Cambium layer is a layer of cells found just under the bark of a plant. These cells produce the growing tissues of a stem, root or leaf. The cambium layer is vital for the distribution of water and nutrients.

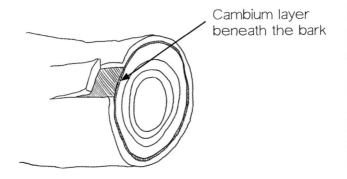

Cambium layer beneath the bark

Rootstock is a plant on which other varieties or cultivars of plants are grafted and which provides the root basis for the grafted tree. Rootstocks are chosen for particular soil types, climates and pest and disease resistance (see section on rootstocks on pages 28–30).

The easiest types of budding and grafting for the home gardener to try are:
- T-budding
- Chip budding
- Whip-and-tongue graft

You will need a bit of equipment to get the best results. The best tools are a budding knife and a very good pair of secateurs. These must be kept clean and razor sharp for grafting. Budding knives will have only one side of the blade sharp to avoid any ripping of bark. Some gardeners use a pocketknife, which is also acceptable, but the job is easier with a budding knife.

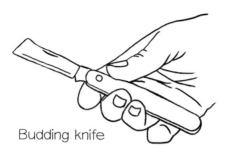

Budding knife

The next item on the shopping list is grafting tape (also called budding tape) – used to totally seal the graft, prevent moisture loss and protect the bud. The tape is left on until the bud shoots away. My mother was a great gardener and often reworked her fruit trees by grafting. For the larger grafts she used to use a rubber glove that was sealed at the top and bottom with butchers string. Necessity is the mother of invention. That was in the days when you had to come up with your own solutions to problems using only what was available. Bloody good use for a rubber glove – better than doing the dishes.

Grafting is all about keeping the cambium layer of the scion in complete contact with the cambium layer of the rootstock, as close together as possible with no air gaps between. And yea verily, the two shall match perfectly and the fruits of your labour shall burst forth (in a year or so – not so much a burst, more of an amble).

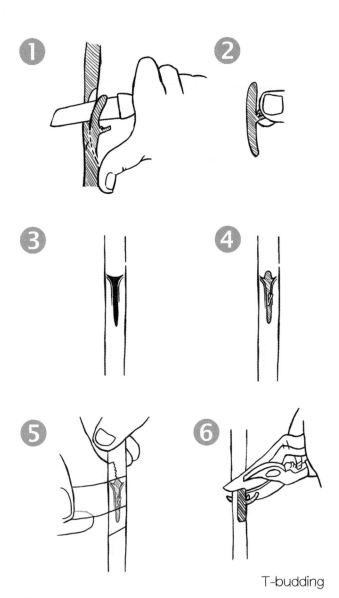

T-budding

T-budding

This is the most common type of grafting for citrus. It is popular because it is easy and you can do multiple bud grafts on the one tree. The best time to bud graft is from early summer through to autumn. Basically you are going to insert a small piece of bark that has a bud into the bark of the rootstock plant. The budwood is very small so a bit of careful handling is needed. Slice the budwood off using either a scalpel or a sharp budding knife (1 and 2).

On the stem of the rootstock (from wood at least two years old), make a T-shaped cut (one horizontal line and the other vertical). The vertical line should be the same length as the budwood (3). Carefully lift the bark back from the rootstock stem and insert the budwood under the bark, making sure the bud sits in the middle of the T cut (4).

This may sound really stupid, but the bud must be the right way up; it should be facing upward. If it is upside down, you have mucked up the whole process and nothing will happen.

Now comes the part where the waves crash on the shore, romantic music is playing and the cambium layers meet. Grafting is all about matching cambium layers and getting them to squeeze together. You might say their romance is budding. Once the bud is inserted into the graft, wrap it tightly with grafting tape (including the bud) to keep the cambium layers in contact (5). Leave the tape on for 3–5 weeks and the bud should have a little spurt of growth. Then remove the tape and prune back the rootstock branch to just above the bud (6).

Chip-budding

Chip-budding can be done nearly all year round. It requires a small piece of bark with a bud from the scion inserted into a small recess on the rootstock. You are going to create an angled chip from the budwood.

Using a grafting knife, cut the budwood from a healthy lateral. Cut at a 30-degree angle running from 1 cm above the bud to 1 cm below. Then make a second cut at a 45-degree angle downwards until this meets with the first cut (1). This will create a wedge-shaped chip (2).

Make similar angled cuts of the same size into the branch or stem of your rootstock (3) and slip the bud chip in (4).

Bind with grafting tape, completely covering the bud chip (5). Leave the grafting tape on for 3–5 weeks (depending on the time of the year – less in spring and summer). You will see the graft has taken when there is callusing around the cut on the rootstock.

Once the graft has taken remove the tape and cut the rootstock branch back to the inserted bud (6). This is important because the bud will not grow if the rootstock stem is left on.

Some gardeners use bubble wrap or a plastic sleeve over the top of the graft to increase the warmth and hasten the time it takes for the graft to seal. Never do this in midsummer in hot temperatures because you will cook the bud. It is, however, a more efficient way of grafting in the cooler months.

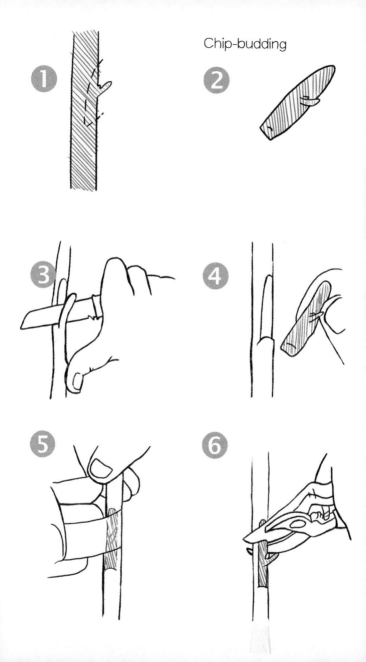

Chip-budding

Whip-and-tongue graft

This is another popular method of grafting for the home gardener, but you will need scion and rootstock with the same diameter. You will be using a stem cutting of the scion that is at least three buds long, and grafting it into a rootstock that has the same diameter so that the cuts you make in one fit into the other.

Make a long sloping cut on both the rootstock stem and the scion stem at a 30-degree angle (1). You will be cutting each stem in the same direction, so that when the scion is sitting upside down on top of the rootstock it becomes a perfect opposite.

Then make a second cut in each stem, running about 2–3 cm deep into the slope in a similar angle to the first cut (2). This will be the tongue (3).

When the stems are joined, the tongue of the scion should fit into the split in the rootstock (4). It sounds complex and you may need to have a few cracks at creating the whip and tongue, but it's a great technique to master.

Wrap the whole grafted area with grafting tape and cut the leaves of the scion in half (5). This reduces transpiration. You can place a plastic sleeve over the entire graft, including the scion leaves, if the weather is cooler.

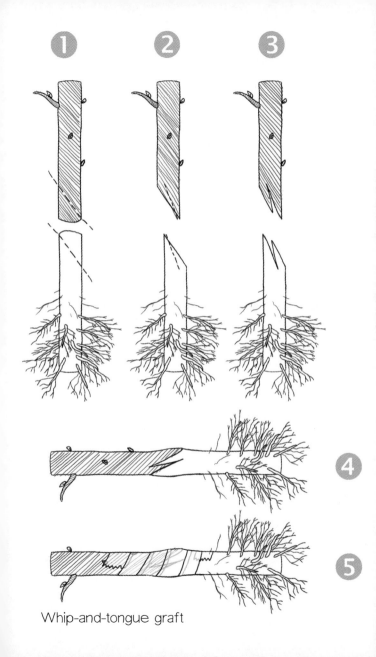

Whip-and-tongue graft

Rootstocks for citrus trees

Nearly all the citrus trees you buy in nurseries will be on a grafted rootstock. That's because different rootstocks perform better in different soil types and climates and are less susceptible to diseases such as phytophthora, tristeza and exocortis. Some rootstocks have a dwarfing effect and others are nematode-resistant (see pests, pages 102–103). Many rootstocks are a cross between two different species of citrus. Your local nursery will supply grafted trees on a rootstock that is most suitable for your area. Only a few varieties of citrus are grown from seed or cuttings.

Benton Citrange *(Poncirus trifoliata x Citrus sinensis)*

The favoured rootstock for Eureka lemon and for areas that experience frosts, but weakens at the knees at any hint of salt. It is resistant to phytophthora and collar rot.

Cleopatra Mandarin *(Citrus reticulata)*

Used extensively for mandarin cultivars, it is resistant to root rot and performs better in heavy soils with loam or clay.

Flying Dragon *(Poncirus trifoliata var. monstrosa)*

Used as a rootstock on many of the dwarf varieties of lemons and limes because of its growth limitations, tolerance of cold winters and disease resistance. It is very thorny, resistant to tristeza virus and thankfully also to nematode attack. Not to be used for Imperial Mandarin grafts.

Rangpur Lime (*Citrus limonia*)

Produces good quality fruit and heavy crops. Used in soils that have a high pH and some degree of salt. It is tristeza virus–resistant.

Rough Lemon (*Citrus jambhiri*)

Can be grown from seed and was used as a rootstock by commercial growers because of its drought tolerance. A bit of a Yin and Yang factor though as it was discovered to be susceptible to nematodes, phytophthora and collar rot. It is only suitable for free-draining soils. The fruit is less juicy and has less sugar. Not suitable as a rootstock for mandarins.

Sweet Orange (*Citrus sinensis*)

Not as resistant to phytophthora or nematodes, but a good rootstock for free-draining soils. It produces a very large tree with heavy crops of juicy fruit. Commonly used for many of the citrus cultivars.

Bitter Orange (*Citrus aurantium*)

This rootstock was used for most of Australia's citrus species but has been found to be susceptible to tristeza virus. If you live in an area that is free of the virus, it's a great rootstock that is very cold and heat-tolerant and produces excellent quality lemons and limes.

Trifoliate Orange (*Poncirus trifoliata*)

If you live in sandy soils with the root-knot nematode present, the citrus you buy from your local nursery will probably be on this rootstock, which is nematode-resistant. Mostly used on lemons now, it will not perform well in arid areas with a high pH or tolerate any salt in the soil or in the water. This rootstock is usually used for pot-grown citrus and delivers very juicy high-quality fruit.

Troyer (*Poncirus trifoliata* hybrid x *Citrus sinensis*)

A tough number that is cold and salt-resistant and was used extensively as the rootstock for Meyer lemons in country areas where other rootstocks struggled. It is also moderately resistant to phytophthora. The fruit grown on this rootstock is apparently very juicy. Troyer rootstock is incompatible for the Eureka lemon.

Planting, watering and fertilising

Citrus trees need an open, sunny site, as the warmth builds up the sugars in the fruit. The more sun the better, with an ideal temperature of 20°C to 32°C. In cooler districts, the best time to plant your young citrus is from September to April – and never in winter. In more tropical or warmer areas you can plant all year round.

The biggest enemies to your citrus trees will be heavy clay soil and severe frosts. If you are unlucky enough to have both of these, I would only grow them in pots. It will save loss of moisture from your body from weeping and wailing. It's soul-destroying to see your lemon tree powering on with lots of new growth, only to be cut in its prime with blackened burnt leaves on the second consecutive week of −5°C.

If you have sandy, gutless soil like much of Western Australia, you will need lots of soil amendments, wetting agents, mulch, liquid and granular fertiliser, perseverance and a strong belief in some higher order of being that keeps you positive for the first few years. You will need to create a well around the tree to capture and hold water.

If you have beautiful loamy soil, regular rainfall, frost-free winters and mild summers I am so jealous I secretly hope your tree develops collar rot.

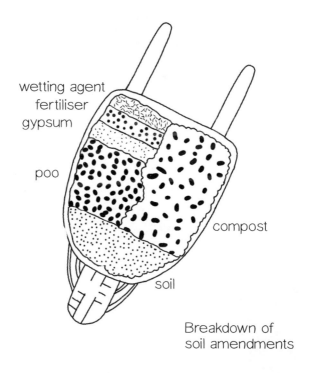

wetting agent
fertiliser
gypsum

poo

compost

soil

Breakdown of
soil amendments

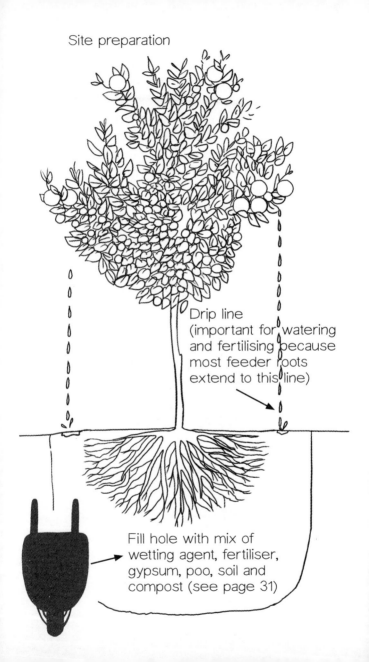

Site preparation

Drip line
(important for watering
and fertilising because
most feeder roots
extend to this line)

Fill hole with mix of
wetting agent, fertiliser,
gypsum, poo, soil and
compost (see page 31)

For the rest of you who have heavy clay soil, creating drainage will be your mantra. You will need clay breaker or gypsum, compost, sharp sand, granular fertiliser, mulch and drainage pipes to move the water. You will need to build up and plant the citrus on a mound to allow water to drain away from the root ball.

Citrus are happiest in soil that has a pH of 6.0–7.0. You can read more on pH levels in soils and how to adjust them on pages 77–79.

Citrus leaves lose a lot of moisture due to transpiration, which is why deep watering rather than shallow is important. During the really hot months apply a polymer coating such as DroughtShield to protect the tree from transpiration stress.

Planting out in sandy soils

There are wonderful soil amendments on the market to help gardeners turn sandy, water-repellent, gutless soils into a medium that grows healthier plants. These include water retention crystals with added nutrients, wetting agents, beneficial microscopic soil bacteria and fungi, fine clay, coco peat, and of course wonderful compost. The better the soil preparation, the stronger and healthier your tree will be.

You will need to determine whether your soil is water-repellent or just gutless, or both. Do not confuse wetting agents with water retention crystals. They perform totally different roles. If you have sandy water-repellent soils you will need both.

Water retention crystals come under names such as water storage crystals, TerraCottem and water tubes. They are really a water-absorbing polymer called a hydrogel – long chains of molecules (called polymers) that absorb incredible amounts of water, releasing the water to plant roots at a later time. The scientific name of this biodegradable chemical is cross-linked polyacrylamide copolymer gel. It's a little bit like carrying those extra kilos on your guts – it gives you something to draw on in times of famine.

Wetting agents are needed for sandy soils, for soils with a high amount of organic matter and for potting mixes, which will otherwise dry out and become hydrophobic. They work by breaking down the waxy coating on soil particles so that the water can penetrate and be absorbed. Wetting agents are usually made up of one or two surfactants that reduce the surface tension of the water and allow water to enter the particle.

In sandy soils, always plant trees out into a well so that the water collects and is directed to the root zone, rather than running off.

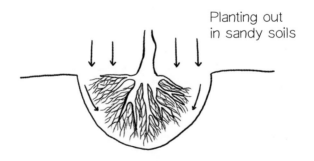

Planting out
in sandy soils

1. Dig a hole twice the width and depth of the pot (or of the root ball, if it's a transplanted tree). This will be a shallow basin into which the tree will be planted.
2. In bottom of hole mix 1 bag compost, ½ bag manure, 4 cups bentonite clay, 1 cup slow-release fertiliser, 1 handful dolomite lime, ½ cup granular wetting agent.
3. Fill hole with water and allow to drain. Repeat.
4. Plant tree with its base entering the soil at the same level as it was in the pot and infill hole with the same mix as used in step 2.
5. Apply a good mulch 5 cm thick, keeping it away from the trunk.
6. Sprinkle 1 cup blood and bone on top of the mulch.
7. Water thoroughly.

Planting out in heavy soils

The biggest concern for citrus in heavy soils is drainage. The soil will be sticky, thick, prone to compaction and hard to work. The roots of plants cannot access oxygen, which impedes growth.

Clay soils can be greatly improved by adding organic matter, sand and gypsum (calcium nitrate). The best mulch for citrus trees is lupin, lucerne, pea straw or sugarcane.

Plants will grow much better if they are raised above ground level in heavy clay soils. Mounding allows the water to run off, rather than sit around the root zone.

Before you make your mound, you will need to break up the surrounding soil.

1. Water the ground so that some implement may penetrate the clay without throwing out your shoulder joint.
2. Attempt to dig a hole with a crowbar, post-hole digger, industrial diamond-tipped spade, and eventually opt for a bobcat with an auger attached.
3. Fill the hole with a mixture of ½ bag potting mix, ½ bag compost, 2 cups gypsum, ½ bag manure, 1 cup slow-release fertiliser.
4. Build a mound made up of two thirds of the above mix, and one third of the soil you have dug out.
5. Plant the tree into the mound.
6. Apply a good mulch 5 cm thick, keeping it away from the trunk.
7. Sprinkle 1 cup blood and bone on top of the mulch.
8. Water lightly.
9. Sit down to rest with a well-earned drink and contact a physio to put your shoulder back into place.

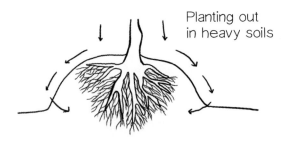

Planting out in heavy soils

Citrus trees have many surface roots. The tree absorbs most of its nutrients through these feeder roots, so any nearby root competition – like plants or lawn – will upset your citrus. You'll need to clear at least a 2-metre diameter around the tree. If you want to grow something under your citrus, make it shallow-rooting herbs like thyme, oregano or sage.

Watering

Regular watering from flower bud stage to fruit set is vital. The roots of citrus are concentrated in the top fifty centimetres of soil, so the priority is to keep moisture in this zone from September to April. You should water either early in the morning or at night, and to the root system only. If you live near the coast, it's advisable to also hose down the leaves once a fortnight to wash off salt deposits from coastal winds.

A 2-metre tree will need about 100 litres of water per month from November through to March. This amount should increase as the tree grows. A 4-metre tree will need 300–400 litres of water per month over the same period.

Water quality is fateful to citrus. Citrus trees don't tolerate salt and are the first plant indicators of the presence of salt-affected soils or salty water. If you have water that has a high pH or salt, it is better to use a drip system so that water particles do not hit the foliage. There are products that can help capture salt and release water. New products like Bactivate, a microbial soil conditioner containing five live strains of beneficial bacteria, restore soil back to its natural balance and aid in the absorption of salt. TerraCottem is another soil conditioner, which many rural local councils use to get trees established in salt-affected areas. It captures the salt in soil and releases water.

Fertilising

Gardeners often get terribly excited when they see fruit developing on their citrus and decide to reward the tree with the only bit of fertiliser it has seen for twelve months. Great handfuls of fertiliser are tossed on with gay abandon. Unfortunately, rather than being grateful for the attention, the citrus tree will respond by dropping all its leaves and most of its fruit.

A little-and-often approach is what your citrus needs. Remember it's the spoilt child of the garden and loves regular attention. Citrus trees need a fertiliser with a ratio of around 10 per cent nitrogen (N), 4 per cent phosphorus (P) and 6 per cent potassium (K), plus trace elements. In the first year, apply half a handful every month from September to February. Stop fertilising altogether from February to autumn to harden up leaf growth and so make the tree less susceptible to citrus leaf miner and frost damage. Spring and early summer are the critical times for fruit production, and the way a tree is looked after at this time will determine the size and quality of the fruit.

Feeder roots on citrus are found on the outer drip line of the canopy of the tree (see page 32). Never dig around this area; the tree will sulk for weeks after – that's what princess plants do. That's the reason we also don't plant around the base of a citrus – they don't like root disturbance and competition from other plants. The best thing to plant under your citrus is nothing – just mulch.

All citrus respond well to foliar feeding when they are putting on new growth. There are many liquid fertilisers on the market, but I prefer to use organic fish-based fertilisers with added seaweed solution. Put this into a spray bottle and spray the whole canopy in the morning, but only on days below 34°C (the nitrogen content in some liquid fertilisers can burn the foliage on hotter days). If you like to create your own liquid fertiliser or compost tea – try this recipe.

Liquid Fertiliser Recipe

Fill to ¾ level a 50-litre plastic bin that has a lid. In it, mix:

- 3 shovels compost
- 1 shovel manure (any type: chicken, sheep, elephant, llama)
- 250 ml seaweed solution
- Cover and let the mix brew for 2 weeks, stirring daily.

In a spray bottle, dilute mixture with water at the ratio of 1:10 and use on foliage and in soil.

Question: Why do our grandparents put Epsom salts on their citrus?

Answer: Epsom salts are a very soluble form of magnesium sulfate and contain magnesium, sulfur and oxygen. Magnesium enables a plant to produce chlorophyll molecules, so it is an essential mineral for healthy leaves. Originally the salts came from natural springs in Epsom in Surrey, England. They are also used in footbaths because magnesium is absorbed in the skin to reduce inflammation.

Pruning and shaping

There's more than one reason to prune citrus trees, and it's not all to do with looks. Fruit production and quality will be much better with regular pruning. Most of the fruit is carried on the outer ninety centimetres of the tree so the best shape to collect fruit is an upright tapering canopy.

With regular pruning it's possible to keep your citrus tree around 4 metres tall and 3 metres wide. The best time to prune is after the spring harvest, or August for those in frost-prone areas. This will give you early summer growth and allow the leaves to harden off before the main heat.

Harsh pruning techniques are better suited to lemons so if you have an overgrown lemon tree, go to town with the chainsaw. And yes, you can prune as hard as Pete Cundall, but only every five or six years. Remember that citrus trees get sunburnt, so after a heavy prune paint the trunk and exposed branches with a white water-based house paint. Always water and fertilise your citrus after pruning to encourage new growth.

For the pruning enthusiast your toolkit should have a pole pruner, long-handled pruners, secateurs, a curved pruning saw and a bow saw. And fellas, you do not have to race out and buy a chainsaw – it is possible to prune without power tools.

Revamping an old, neglected citrus tree

If you've inherited a garden and there are neglected citrus trees that you would like to bring back to life, here's a foolproof method, but do it only in spring, autumn or late summer.

- Prune tree by 50 per cent
- Dig a trench that is 20 cm deep and 20 cm wide around the circumference of the tree's new drip line (see page 32)
- Fill the trench with a mix of soil amendments (see page 31) and water well

The feeder roots will sniff out all that good tucker and will grow new shoots in a matter of weeks.

Transplanting

Citrus trees respond well to being transplanted if you do the preparation correctly and give them TLC until they fully recover. The best time to move them is in spring after the frosts, or early autumn after the heat. If you live in a mild-summer region, you can shift them during late summer. Have everything ready to go to make the process as quick as possible. You should soak the tree thoroughly with water every day for 2 weeks prior to moving so that the soil stays attached to the root system.

1. First prepare the hole into which the citrus is moving. Make sure it is wider and deeper than the root mass that is being dug up.
2. Add to the hole soil amendments like compost, sea-weed solution, wetting agent and half a bag of sheep manure. Water the hole well and allow it to drain.
3. Prune back the tree that is being transplanted by a third. Some branches may need to be cut back completely to the trunk. Think about the shape of the tree and maintain a balanced look. Make sure all cuts are at an angle.
4. Make a note of the orientation of the tree (before transplanting) and mark on the trunk where it faces west. You will be planting it at the same degree when it's transplanted to prevent sunburn on the trunk and stems.
5. Remove any remaining fruit from the tree, regardless of size.
6. Spray remaining foliage with DroughtShield, which will help reduce transplant shock due to transpiration.
7. Dig around the tree getting as much root ball as possible and keeping in mind it will need to be carried into its new position. If you have a large tree (taller than 3 metres) you may need a backhoe, a Dingo or other machinery to move it. A root ball of around 3 metres will be needed for a large tree. For smaller trees, dig a trench that is 50 cm deep around the outer part of the drip line, severing all the roots. Dig underneath one side of

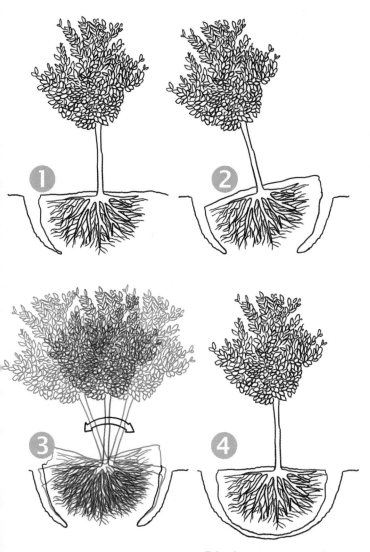

Digging out a small
citrus tree (Step 7)

the root mass first (1), lean the tree over towards this side and then dig out the other side (2). Rock the tree back and forth until the root ball comes away from the soil (3). When you have completed the digging you should have an actual ball of roots and soil (4).

8. Trim all the jagged edges of the roots with a clean pair of secateurs.

9. Slide a tarpaulin, old carpet or piece of wood underneath the root ball to enable you to drag it into its new hole or put it onto machinery, a ute or a trailer.

10. Plant the tree into the new hole, using a mixture of compost, soil and water during the infill stage to prevent big air gaps. Cover the root ball with soil. Make sure the tree is facing the same direction as it was before transplanting.

11. Stake the tree until it forms new roots, which will take around a year.

12. Drench the soil in a seaweed solution and do this once every 3 weeks. The foliage can also be sprayed once a month with seaweed solution or weak compost tea.

13. If substantial foliage is lost in the transplanting process, erect a shade hat that goes over the tree for the first summer. Use 40–50 per cent shade cloth and remove it as soon as the weather cools down.

14. Do not fertilise the transplanted tree until it starts shooting new leaves.

Growing citrus in pots

Citrus trees grow very well in containers and can be kept for over fifty years in pots. This is dependent on having a strong back, or friends and family with strong backs, because there'll be a fair bit of moving to keep them warm all year round.

Citrus trees originally came from South-East Asia and are largely tropical to subtropical trees. If you live in frost-prone areas, only grow them in a pot and move them to a warm position out of the frost line in winter. Definitely buy yourself a trolley with wide wheels, as you will be doing this chore every year. Either that or build yourself a large glasshouse and call it an orangery. A trolley will be substantially cheaper.

When selecting a pot for your citrus choose one with a capacity of at least 50 litres. Your tree will be happy in that pot for quite a few years, but you will need to top it up with compost and mulch from time to time. Eventually you will need a pot that's around 100 litres. Good drainage is vital, so line the bottom of the pot with about 4 cm of blue metal and raise the pot off the ground with either bricks or little feet (not your dog's).

If you want to get the most out of your citrus, planting it in good quality potting mix alone is not enough. Potting mixes can become water-repellent over a period of time, and ants can crawl up through the base and burrow in the soil around the root system. I prefer to make up my own cake mix for fruit trees that has a bit more oomph.

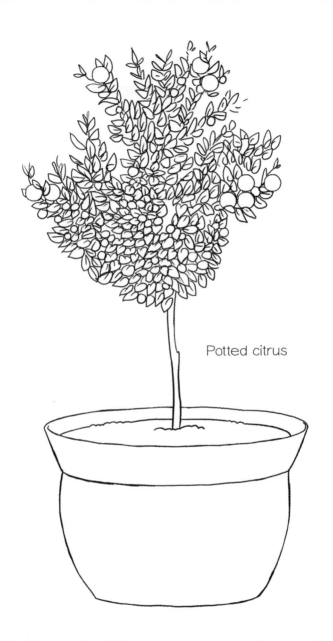

Potted citrus

In a wheelbarrow, mix together:

- 2 bags good quality potting mix
- ½ bag compost
- 2 handfuls bentonite clay
- 2 handfuls organic-based fertiliser with trace elements
- 2 handfuls granular wetting agent

Leave room at the top of the pot for mulch, which will need to be 5 cm thick. During flowering and fruiting, pot-grown citrus require liquid fertiliser in the form of fish or crustacean emulsion poured over the leaves and into the soil. Use this in combination with a seaweed-based solution that conditions the soil.

Varieties of citrus suitable for pots

- All limes, including the bush tucker limes and Kaffir lime
- All kumquats
- Calamondin
- Dwarf grapefruit – Honneffs Surprise
- Dwarf kumquat – Nagami
- Dwarf lemon – Flying Dragon
- Dwarf mandarin – Afourer; Daisy; Emperor; Flying Dragon; Freemont; Honey Murcott; Okitsu Wase; Pixie
- Dwarf orange – Cara Cara; Flying Dragon; Hamlin; Lanes Late; Valencia; Valencia Seedless; Washington Navel
- Dwarf tangelo – Minneola
- Lots-a-Lemons
- Splitzer varieties

Pruning a standard shape in pots

1. First year: prune lower branches by one third (also known as an underprune).
2. Second year: cut 10 cm off the top branch and remove all lower branches at the trunk.
3. Third year onwards: select only four main laterals and remove others as this will be the framework of the tree. Tip-prune once a year.

Pruning in the first, second and third years

Citrus varieties for the home gardener

In the varieties lists that follow, the months in brackets represent the fruit harvest period. Although the ripening and harvest periods can vary depending on climate, this is a fair indication for most gardens along the Australian coastline. A good tip is to ask your local nursery about the variety's ripening times in your area.

Oranges (Citrus sinensis and Citrus aurantium)

It is not known where the sweet orange originally came from, but it is believed to be in the area bordered by northern India, Burma and southern China. India and China are still today some of the world's biggest producers of oranges. The orange is a beautiful medium-sized tree that reaches 8–10 metres in height. Oranges are more cold-tolerant and more compact than lemons. They have the most alluring perfume and will carry flowers and fruit on the tree for some time: it can take up to a year for a crop to ripen. This is a truly rewarding fruit tree that is worthy of a place in any garden.

Orange trees are remarkably tough in hot climates. In Seville in Spain they are used extensively as street trees and grow magnificently in temperatures from 40°C to –3°C. The bitter orange is Seville's favoured street tree and it is also grown as a hedging plant, covering giant walls and espaliered against houses. The hardiness of the tree is amazing. The perfume in the streets is sumptuous.

All orange trees need full sun and deep well-draining soil with a neutral pH. They have a shallow root system so place a thick layer of lupin, lucerne, pea straw or sugarcane mulch that goes out as far as the drip line. Feed them with an organic fertiliser with trace elements at the beginning of each season. Remove lower branches at the trunk to prevent fruit touching the soil, and prune after harvest. Do not prune orange trees harshly as the wood is susceptible to sunburn.

The navels

Cara Cara (April–August)

A newish variety in Australia hailing from Venezuela in the 1970s, Cara Cara is the first to fruit in spring. The flesh is pink and sweet. A small-growing tree suitable for courtyards and pots.

Delta (June–October)

A seedless variety with less acidic fruit on a medium-sized tree.

Lanes Late Navel (September–December)

A variation of the Washington Navel, named after a Mr Lindsay Lane from whose property in New South Wales this tree was selected. The fruit matures 3 months later than the Washington Navel and will remain on the tree up to Christmas. It is thin-skinned with large, deep-orange fruit and seedless flesh. The tree is medium-sized and performs well in mild climates.

Leng Navel (May–September)
An excellent, sweet, juicy orange with all the traits of the Washington Navel such as shedding its crop. It was discovered on the Leng property in Victoria in 1934.

Navelina (May–September)
A lovely Spanish variety that likes hot summers and cold winters, and a reliable cropper with slightly smaller fruit. The tree is compact and its fruit naturally develops an outstanding deep red-orange skin.

Rohde (May–August)
A sweet navel variety that grows well in dry inland areas with hot summers and cold winters. Fruit does not stay on the tree long.

Washington Navel (May–September)
An early-fruiting tree with large, almost seedless oranges that are sweet and juicy. The downside of the Washington Navel is its habit of shedding fruit just before ripening, and of occasionally developing branches that produce inferior fruit – either very seedy or bitter. It is, however, the most cold-tolerant of all citrus.

Common oranges

Hamlin (June–August)

A very old orange, and from 1897 classified as a cultivar of *Citrus sinensis*. It has an upright habit and produces thin-skinned yellow-orange fruit that is almost seedless. It is cold-tolerant and prefers cooler summers.

Joppa (October–September)

Has the distinction of being one of the orange varieties that arrived with the First Fleet. This orange had a revival in the 1940s because it's great for juicing and eating. The fruit holds well on the tree and it will adapt nicely to different climates.

Midnight Seedless (June–September)

An early-maturing seedless orange with very thin rind and excellent quality fruit.

Seedless Valencia (October–December)

As the name suggests it is seedless, but only if it is not planted close to a seeded variety. The Seedless Valencia fruits 1–2 months later than Valencia.

Valencia (September–December)

The Valencia is probably the most popular orange tree in Australian backyards. It is the queen of juicing oranges and the fruit lasts for months on the tree, taking up to a year to ripen. This means the tree will have new fruit developing at the same time as mature fruit is ready for harvest. All this takes so much energy it's no wonder they crop better in alternate years. In subtropical climates the fruit may return to a green colour if on the tree too long, but this doesn't affect the taste. Valencias need lots of heat so pick a spot that can retain the heat in winter.

Blood oranges

Arnold Blood (September–January)

A great Blood variety for the tropics with deep-red flesh that is very juicy.

Blood (September–January)

Distinctive mild-flavoured fruit with red colour in the skin or flesh. The red colour develops best in dry, hot climates with cold nights. The fruit are smaller than Valencias and the tree more compact. Grows well in pots.

Maltese Blood (September–January)

Grows well in hot, dry regions and is suitable for both juicing and eating. The blood pigmentation will not develop in tropical or cool areas. Now available on dwarf rootstock.

Bitter oranges

Bergamot (July–August)

If you are seriously into Earl Grey tea, plant one of these oranges, as it's the secret ingredient that gives the tea its distinctive flavour and smell. The Bergamot orange (*Citrus bergamia*) is really a dwarf form of the Seville orange and is grown on a large scale in Italy for the production of bergamot oil. The distilled oil from the flowers is an important component of many perfumes. This orange will not tolerate heavy, wet soils and requires more water in summer than most oranges. It is suitable for semi-tropical regions.

Chinotto (June–August)

You have probably had the drink called Chinotto or perhaps been lucky enough to sit on a terrace in Tuscany in Italy and sip a Campari and ice. Welcome to the fabulous little shrub the Italians call Chinotto (the scientific name is *Citrus myrtifolia*). The fruit is extremely tart and the shrub very slow-growing and compact, reaching a height of around 4 metres. In late spring masses of flowers fill the air with their fragrance and the fruit is ready to harvest in winter. It grows well in a pot.

Red Seville (July–August)

A smooth-skinned variety of the Seville with larger and flatter fruit than the Rough Seville. The skin colour is red and the juice incredibly bitter. It makes for a great shade tree with its wide canopy.

Rough Seville (everbearing)

A favourite fruit for marmalade with thick, pebbled skin and small apple-shaped fruit. It copes with extremes of temperatures and it fruits and flowers on and off all year round.

Seville (July–August)

The classic variety of *Citrus aurantium*. This citrus adorns the streets of Seville in Spain, and in my book is one of the most hard-working, exquisitely fragrant oranges you could want. Recorded in Arabia by the ninth century, they were part of the landscape in Seville by the twelfth century. Sir Walter Raleigh transported some Seville Oranges to England in 1595, but they died during the bitter winter that gripped England and Europe in 1739. The Seville Orange is an incredibly hardy tree that grows up to 6 metres, and its sour oranges are used mostly for marmalade. The fruit is apple-shaped and yellowish. For those who live in frost-prone areas, the Seville Orange is fabulous. They should be grown a lot more in Australia, as they are both drought and frost-hardy.

Yuzu (June–August)

A very old Chinese citrus (*Citrus junos*) that looks similar to a grapefruit. The fruit is rarely eaten raw but used to make vinegar and sauces. In Japan it is the key ingredient in yuzu kosho, the spicy sauce made from the zest plus chilli and salt. Yuzu is cold-tolerant and will grow in frost areas up to −5°C.

Lemons (Citrus limon)

When I was a kid, just about every backyard had a lemon tree. They are such rewarding trees. Deep, glossy evergreen leaves, pink flushed white perfumed flowers and an abundance of fruit on and off all year round. You could not find a better evergreen tree for your garden, which may account for the fact that there are very few lemon trees grown commercially.

Citrus limon originates from India, the Himalayas, Burma or southern China, depending on who you read. One thing that is known is that they are highly adaptable to climate and soil type as long as it's free-draining. They can grow into large trees – up to 8 metres tall and 6 metres wide. All varieties need full sun, enriched soil and regular applications of trace elements. Lemons are hungry feeders with a shallow root system, so mulching and fertilising are important factors in maintaining the tree's health and fruit production.

Lemons have no salt tolerance at all and are susceptible to phytophthora. Prune your lemon tree so that you can reach the fruit, and remove some branches on the inside so that sunlight can penetrate into the canopy. Some lemons flower and fruit all year round so it's difficult to know when to prune. Long, vigorous watershoots can be pruned anytime, but in cooler climates prune after the threat of frosts has disappeared.

Fruit can take up to 7–9 months to ripen depending on variety and climate and you will have flowers and fruit on the tree at the same time. Most lemons are grown on grafts but make sure you select the right rootstock to suit both your soil type and climate (see section on rootstocks, pages 28–30).

Eureka (everbearing)
Large, thornless, heavy-bearing tree suited to warmer

climates. The fruit is large and rougher-skinned than the Lisbon, but of excellent quality. Eureka fruits nearly all year round with its main crops in spring and summer. If you want a tart lemon with a high juice content, this is the one.

Fino (June–October)

A large tree with thin-skinned seedless fruit. It will fruit on and off all year in tropical climates and has a tendency to grow thorns.

Lemonade (everbearing)

It's my favourite little lemon because of its small and abundant fruit. The lemons have a mild lemon flavour and smooth skin. Perhaps it's a cross between a mandarin and a lemon. It will throw out a few thorns, but the fruit has such a lovely flavour that it's worth the odd prick. The fruit is thin-skinned and you can peel it just like an orange.

Lisbon (everbearing)

An Aussie lemon since the mid 1800s. Prolific cropper on a dense, vigorous, often thorny tree. The Prior Lisbon is less thorny. The fruit is thin-skinned and sumptuous, with a distinctive nipple on the end. Lisbon has its heaviest crop in winter but fruits again in spring and summer. It is extremely cold-tolerant.

Lots-a-Lemons (everbearing)

Related to the Meyer lemon, this small shrub grows to only 2 metres in height. Grown from cuttings, it is better suited to pots than in the ground because of its disease vulnerability. The lemons are thin-skinned and sweet but susceptible to fruit fly.

Meyer (June–July)

A small to medium-sized tree that produces most of its fruit in winter and makes up for a short fruiting period with sheer quantity. The fruit is sweet and juicy and mostly seedless. It may be a cross between a lemon and an orange, which would account for its smooth skin and sweeter fruit. It is the most cold-tolerant of the lemon varieties.

Villa Franca (everbearing)

Closely related to Eureka, both the fruit and the tree look similar but Villa Franca crops more heavily in summer. It is a vigorous tree with thorns that grows well in both dry inland regions and tropical regions.

Limes (various species and hybrids)

All limes require free-draining soil and lots of sunshine. They grow very well in pots and need ample summer watering to prevent fruit drop (see page 122). Limes need protection from strong winds as this will affect fruit formation or cause fruit drop. Water-stress around flowering time could cost you your whole crop. Always apply a mulch to keep the root system moist. Never prune during summer as the wood is susceptible to sunburn which can in turn promote disease.

Kaffir

Citrus hystrix. Grown for the leaves, not the rough, bumpy, weird-looking fruit, which is virtually inedible. Its white flowers are highly fragrant. Kaffir lime is native to Indonesia and its leaves are used extensively in South-East Asian cooking. If you make your own tom yum goong soup, grow this tree in a pot. Use the fully mature leaves in the kitchen as these have more oils. In parts of Asia the fruit is boiled up and the pulp is used as a hair rinse.

Kaffir limes are tropical plants and hate the cold. They will not survive frosts. They are easy to grow from cuttings or you can aerial-layer them in late spring or summer. Only tip-prune them and encourage a bushy habit. They are great in pots as the tree only grows to 3–5 metres. A word of warning: Kaffirs are thorny little devils. Most are now grafted but seed-grown ones will have lots of variation, particularly the number of thorns on stems.

Key (everbearing)

A thornless version of the West Indian lime and the main ingredient in key lime pie – the official pie of the American state of Florida.

Krusea (everbearing)

A yellow fruiting version of the Rangpur lime with a very mild flavour. The tree and the fruit are quite small, making it ideal for pot cultivation.

Rangpur (everbearing)

Citrus limonia. Originating in India, this cold-tolerant lime is great for pots. It has more of a mandarin flavour, with acidic, seedy fruit that ranges from pale-green to red or orange. It will fruit most of the year and the new growth has a lovely purple tinge. You can successfully grow the Rangpur from seed and it will fruit in four years.

Tahitian (July–August)

Citrus latifolia. A small evergreen tree (up to 6 metres) that produces fruit on and off all year round in tropical climates. In cooler climates more fruit appear in winter. The fruit is like a small lemon, with smooth yellow skin and pale-green flesh, that is seedless and very juicy. The most cold-tolerant of limes but the cold will abate its growth. Pick the fruit green a few weeks before it ripens fully.

West Indian (everbearing)

Citrus aurantifolia. A small tree (up to only 4 metres) that will produce fruit all year round in warm climates. The fruit is smaller than the Tahitian lime with a few seeds but a wonderful tangy flavour and aroma. The skin is a glossy green colour with green-yellow flesh. This lime should only be grown in warmer climates. Its sensitivity to cold also affects the fruit: if stored in the refrigerator, they shrivel up and lose flavour very quickly. The West Indian lime is very thorny and is often used as a burglar and animal-deterrent hedge. Pruning of course could be a little tricky, but a pair of long-handled pruners may save some tears.

Bush tucker or native limes

(various species and hybrids)

Thankfully substantial numbers of native limes are making their way into many of our gardens. Some are small shrubs, some are large trees with sweetly perfumed white flowers and sharp thorns. The fruit is small and can be round, oval or elongated. Its colour ranges from white to pink, red and pale yellow. The skin is fine and you will not be able to peel them – a bit like kumquats – so you eat the whole fruit. It's the skin that has all the flavour, so grating them may be near on impossible unless you fancy leaving pieces of your finger in the meal.

There is still much research to be done on varieties and cultivars of native lime trees. Their genetic diversity is enormous, making it hard for breeders and growers to find the best form for the commercial market.

Native limes are much sought after in restaurants for their zesty, sharp flavour. They lend themselves very well to Asian food and make fabulous sauces and dressings. Choose the right native lime for your region: some originate from rainforests and others from the desert. Some will grow in the shade and others need full sun.

There is no need to prune any of the native limes (except tip-prune to encourage new growth) but do take out dead wood. This can be carried out any time of the year. Native limes will be susceptible to most of the insects that attack other citrus, but the main disease to affect them is melanose – a fungal disease causing brown spotting on the fruit, foliage and stems. Pruning any dead stems and thinning out the canopy will help control the disease.

All native limes are slow-growing, but they will fruit in their third year. They need excellent drainage and respond best to slow-release organic fertilisers and compost-enriched soil. They will all grow exceptionally well in pots.

It is difficult to know the fruiting time of many of the native limes as variation is enormous and they are sensitive to changes in soil and temperature. If you are growing them, keep a diary of flowering and fruiting.

Australian Blood

A hybrid of Red Finger lime and Rangpur lime (*Citrus australasica* var. *sanguinea* × *Citrus limonia*). The hybrid is produced by open pollination, from the pollen of Red Finger lime and the seedling form of the Rangpur lime. The fruit is round, red and tangy.

Australian Sunrise

Grows to 2–4 metres, bearing small, yellow, pear-shaped fruit. A hybrid from an open-pollinated seedling selected from a faustrimedin (*Citrus australasica* × [*Fortunella* sp. × *Citrus reticulata* 'Calamondin']), which is a hybrid of the Finger lime and the Calamondin, itself a hybrid between the kumquat and a variety of the mandarin group (*Citrus reticulata*). The fruit looks identical to an oval-shaped kumquat. This lime has a tendency to die back on the branches, but if you can get them to the fourth year they tend to lose that trait.

Australian Outback

A selection of *Citrus glauca*, it has been bred to be thornless with long yellow fruit 3 cm in length that ripens in summer. It is tolerant of drought, salt and frost.

Desert

Citrus glauca. Grows to 2–4 metres and bears small, seedless green to yellow fruit. It is native to Queensland and New South Wales, west of a line running from Rockhampton to Dubbo, with some isolated occurrences in central South Australia. The Desert lime will tolerate alkaline soils and is drought, frost and salt-tolerant. Probably child-tolerant as well because it has many thorns.

Finger

Citrus australasica. Grows to 6 metres in rainforest, but probably half that height in other areas and bears oblong green to yellow fruit. Native to rainforests in southern Queensland and northern New South Wales. Finger limes are prickly little devils and in the wild they show a great diversity of shape and form. The finger-like fruit is about 11 cm long and when the fruit is opened it resembles something out of a sci-fi movie. Little caviar-like crystals appear and literally burst from the fruit.

Because they are at home in the rainforests as an understorey plant, I suggest they wouldn't be frost-tolerant and would require ample summer water and protection from the hot sun and also from hot or cold winds.

Rainforest Pearl

A cultivar of the Red Finger lime, *Citrus australasica* var. *sanguinea*, this is an open, upright small tree to 3 metres, bearing yellow-green fruit with red pulp at maturity. Requires ample summer watering and mulching. The flesh is pink or crimson. Plant in a protected position.

Round

Citrus Australis. Grows 3–10 metres, with rough-skinned green to yellow fruit. Native to the rainforest margins of south-east Queensland, from Brisbane northwards. It is very adaptable and grows well in arid areas with alkaline soils.

Mandarins (Citrus reticulata)

The most popular citrus as far as kids are concerned because the fruit is so easy to peel. Mandarins are trickier to grow than other citrus but they are adaptable to many different climates – apart from the tropics where they can develop fungal diseases. Do not plant two or more different varieties of mandarin that flower at the same time, or cross-pollination will cause your seedless variety to produce seed. If you are planning an orchard, there are early, mid and late-season varieties that will prevent this problem.

Mandarins like to be fed often. They are greedy buggers and prefer a well-balanced fertiliser with all the trace elements. Never fertilise during flowering – you will lose a lot of fruit due to the stress caused by the plant trying to absorb nitrogen. Too much nitrogen also causes very puffy-skinned fruit.

It's best to pick the fruit over a period of 6 weeks as it ripens because the fruit does not keep very well on the tree. Apply a thick mulch of pea straw, lupin, lucerne or sugarcane to prevent heat and water stress.

Afourer (May–July)

A selected cultivar from Morocco, this is a vigorous tree with medium-sized fruit, puffy skin and a low seed count.

Avana Tardivo (August–October)

A vigorous tree bearing small, seedy fruit with loads of juice. A popular mandarin in Italy.

Clementine (April–June)

Originally from the Mediterranean, this mandarin is a hybrid of a tangerine and the wild orange of North Africa and does well in warm temperate climates. These mandarins are the most popular (along with Imperial) because they are virtually seedless. Be careful not to plant seeded mandarin varieties together with Clementines as they will cross-pollinate and both will eventually produce fruit with lots of seeds. Clementines will crop in alternate years so it's best to heavy-prune during the light-cropping year to encourage even cropping and higher-quality fruit.

Ellendale (July–August)

Large fruit with seeds but delicious flavour. A vigorous,

spreading tree that bears so much fruit it has a tendency to snap branches. It is suitable for cold climates and inland areas.

Emperor (July–August)
So called because it may have come to Australia with the Chinese during the early gold-rush years. A mandarin with an excellent flavour, loose skin and large, almost seedless fruit. Pick the fruit as it ripens because it doesn't last well on the tree.

Fina (May–June)
Good flavour, with small, pale coloured fruit.

Freemont (July–September)
Beautiful flavour, deep orange-red skin with very juicy fruit, but can be seedy and thick-skinned. A prolific bearer suitable for subtropical climates.

Hickson (June–August)
An improved form of the Ellendale mandarin with fewer seeds and thinner skin. The fruit is easy to peel and grows well in subtropical regions.

Honey Murcott (August–October)
A tropical, warm-climate mandarin that adapts to cooler climates. It has medium-sized sweet flesh that is almost iridescent orange. The fruit has many seeds and can be hard to peel.

Imperial (April–July)

A hybrid discovered at Emu Plains property in New South Wales with easy-peeling sweet, tangy, small fruit, very few seeds and thin skin. The tree is vigorous and produces more fruit than it can carry. On its heavier bearing years, remove up to 70 per cent of the fruit.

Kara (August–October)

Yields juicy fruit that is almost seedless and peels easily. The tree is a bit scraggly and will need pruning in the early years to get a good shape.

Murcott (August–September)

A late-season flavoursome mandarin with very large, sweet, juicy, bright-orange fruit but lots of seeds. It over-crops and needs heavy thinning to prevent branches breaking.

Marisol (April–May)

Yields well, with good-sized, juicy fruit.

Nules (May–June)

A Clementine variety. Better flavour than Marisol with good-sized fruit.

Satsuma (May–June)

Great mandarin for the cold-climate garden. The tree is small to medium-sized and produces seedless, thin-skinned fruit with a mild, sweet flavour and orange flesh. There are many Satsuma varieties available. If you're in a colder part of Australia a good variety for you is Okitsu Wase (April–June) which adapts to just about any climate. Its fruit is flat, seedless and easy to peel.

Tangerine (October–December)

Very closely related to the mandarin, and indeed some references label tangerine as a subspecies of the mandarin. Some people refer to all things small and orange as tangerines, but the generic name is actually mandarin, and tangerine is only a mandarin variety. The tangerine tree is thornless with long weeping branches. Fruit is bright orange and very juicy. The skin is not as loose as some mandarin varieties but easier to peel than oranges. Tangerines tend to be biennial croppers.

Grapefruits (Citrus paradisi)

Grapefruit trees can grow to around 7 metres in height and 4 metres in width. They have a distinctive winged leafstalk on their leaves and outstanding perfumed flowers. The leafstalk is a good way of identifying your tree if you're not sure what you've inherited.

Most varieties are thornless and almost seedless. They fruit like a pawpaw tree possessed, having clusters of up to five fruit on each branch. This can be a problem as the weight of the fruit causes branches to break from the tree. The fruit is large and round and can be green, yellow, orange or red depending on the variety. The tree needs free-draining soil and a pH of around 6–7.

Grapefruit are not very cold-tolerant and will curl up

and die in heavy frosts. They need to grow in full sun with long summers. If you live in areas that have a short mild summer, the fruit will be bitter. Grapefruit trees do really well in the tropics and subtropics, but the skin may remain green rather than turn yellow or orange. The fruit will still taste sweet.

Most grapefruit are ready to harvest in autumn or winter. They can take up to 6 months to ripen after flowering and the longer you leave the fruit on the tree, the sweeter it will be.

Prune your grapefruit trees when they are young to develop strong branches to carry the fruit. Never let branches reach the ground, as the fruit will develop diseases. Pruning should take place after harvesting.

Flame (June–September)

A prolific producer and a selected form of the Ruby Red. It has deeper red flesh but also needs tropical or subtropical conditions for the flesh to colour. The skin will remain green even when ripe.

Marsh Seedless (June–September)

An excellent cultivar with thin-skinned, juicy fruit on a medium-sized tree. Flesh is pale yellow and much sweeter in warmer climates. It bears seedless acidic fruit.

Rio Red (June–October)

A cultivar from Texas that performs well in warm climates. A very vigorous (it's Texan) and productive tree with deep-red seedless flesh. The skin has a pink blush.

Ruby Red (June–December)

Improved version of Marsh, with pink-red flesh and a sweeter flavour. You'll only get the red colour developing in hotter climates.

Thompson Seedless (June–September)

Related to Marsh Seedless with blush pink flesh and yellow skin.

Wheeny (June–October)

This grapefruit was not named because of its size but because it was a seedling that popped up at Wheeny Creek in New South Wales. It is a large, spreading tree that will make a great shade tree for a courtyard. The fruit has green-yellow flesh that makes the best juice. It does have lots of seeds but it suits very cold climates.

Pomelos (Citrus maxima)

An old ancestor of the grapefruit, the pomelo is named for the size of its fruit, which can grow as large as 25 cm and weigh 2 kg. If you think you have a tyrannosaurus-sized grapefruit, it is a pomelo. The tree is large as well and grows up to 12 metres in height with a spread of 6 metres.

Pomelo fruit is less bitter than grapefruit but only tastes good in warm climates, and it's not so good for juicing because the rind is about 3 cm thick. This is pretty clever of the tree because pests cannot penetrate through the skin, making pomelos relatively pest-free. The fruit's pink or yellow flesh is very juicy (if not juicable) and the tartness depends on the variety.

Pomelo trees are surprisingly frost and salt-tolerant but unless they have a long hot summer the fruit will rip off the roof of your mouth. Like all other citrus, pomelos require full sun, free-draining soil, ample summer watering and lots of room to grow. Their growth can be a bit unruly, so prune every year after harvest. The branches will definitely need a prop to keep them from snapping with the weight of the fruit. In the tropics, you can expect to harvest up to 100 fruit. The fruit will ripen post-harvest and will last for weeks in the fridge.

Bosworth Pink (June–October)
A heavy bearer with pink-red flesh and bright green skin.

Carters Red (June–October)
Ideally suited to the tropics with rosy pink flesh.

Nam Roi (June–October)
A newcomer from Vietnam with large, juicy, seedless fruit. Suitable for tropical areas. It is also available in dwarf form.

Tahiti (June–October)
One of the thinner-skinned varieties with yellow-green flesh.

Tangelos (Citrus tangelo)

Tangelos are a cross between a tangerine (type of mandarin) and a pomelo (*Citrus reticulata* × *Citrus maxima*) or a tangerine and a grapefruit (*Citrus reticulata* × *Citrus paradisi*). They have soft juicy fruit that peels like a grapefruit but has the juice and flavour of a mandarin. Tangelo trees can grow to 8 metres and are thornless. They are cold-tolerant but not frost-tolerant. The fruit will develop sugars with long, hot summers and will be more tart in cooler climates.

In tropical areas, the skin of the fruit may remain green or will change from orange back to green, but this does not impinge on the flavour.

Minneola (July–September)
A tangerine and grapefruit cross. Vigorous, productive tree bearing deep orange-red fruit rich in juice with a tang of grapefruit. Allow the fruit to fully ripen on the tree to increase sweetness. You will know if you have a Minneola as it has a prominent neck on the top of the fruit. Minneola appears to fruit biennially.

Orlando (June–July)
Like Minneolas, Orlando tangelos are a hybrid of Duncan grapefruit and Dancy tangerine. Orlando performs better than other tangelos in colder climates. The fruit is very juicy with a mandarin taste and grows on a vigorous, productive tree. The downside to Orlando is that you will need two trees for cross-pollination.

San Jacinto (June–July)

This early-season tangelo is better suited to the tropics. It has skin like a mandarin and tart flesh.

Seminole (September–November)

Heavy cropper and medium-sized tree bearing grapefruit-sized fruit with deep-orange skin and a grapefruit tang. It is a very seedy character.

Kumquats (Fortunella spp.)

Kumquats are sweet little trees that only grow to around 3 metres with a 2-metre spread. They have small deep-green leaves and are thornless. Unlike other citrus varieties, the flowers are formed in the leaf axils. The flowers have a sweet perfume and are pure white. Fruit are round or oval and yellow or orange coloured, depending on the species. Some are seedless, others have many seeds.

Kumquats will cross-pollinate with each other, which often causes seedless species to develop seeds. You can grow kumquats from seed; it will take about seven years to flower and fruit. A grafted bought one should fruit within two years. Fruit takes months to ripen. Only pick them when they are fully coloured, otherwise the tartness will stay with you a long time.

The best way to eat kumquats is skin and all because the skin is sweeter than the flesh. Most people use their deliciously tart fruit for marmalade or tarts, but try them straight off the tree – it's a refreshing small treat.

Kumquats are the tough boys on the citrus block. They are frost-tolerant and can cope with heat extremes. They grow well in pots and make a fantastic Christmas tree if you are lucky enough to still have the fruit – ready-made decorations.

I have seen many attractive kumquat hedges, but they require regular pruning. Most people prune them into a lollypop standard and grow them in pots.

Marumi (July–September)

Fortunella japonica. Has round, juicy fruit with a thinner and sweeter skin than the Nagami. It is the most cold-tolerant of the kumquat species.

Meiwa (July–September)

Fortunella crassifolia. Has large, seedless, sweet fruit. If you see a variegated kumquat it will be from this species. Meiwa is the sweetest of the lot.

Nagami (July–September)

Fortunella margarita. The fruit are small, oval-shaped, deep-orange coloured and aromatic. Used mostly for marmalades, candying and preserving.

Calamondins (Citrus madurensis)

Calamondins look very like kumquats but will grow into a larger tree. They are classed as a cross between a mandarin and a kumquat. If you see a variegated kumquat, it is likely to be a calamondin. The small, bright-orange juicy fruit appears from July to December and stays on the tree for months. The skin is easily peeled and breaks into segments just like a mandarin. They are very popular in Asian countries where the juice is made into marinades for fish and chicken dishes. The skin is also dried and used to flavour teas. Calamondins are also great in marmalade or used as a tangy addition to dressings for salads.

Citrons (Citrus medica)

An old species of citrus that grows into a small tree no larger than 5 metres. It is believed that *Citrus medica* is the granddaddy plant of all modern citrus. It certainly has a well-recorded history from Alexander the Great to Pliny the Elder. Also known as the Persian Apple, it was grown for medicinal purposes. The rind was used as an antibiotic and a remedy for seasickness and the juice was mixed into wine and drunk as an antidote to poison. I'm not too sure if this worked or not, but I wouldn't gamble my life on it.

Citrus medica is easily grown from cuttings, which may account for its spread around the world. The fruit is bright yellow with thick fragrant skin that makes wonderful candied peel.

The best-known *Citrus medica* is the weird and wonderful Buddha's Hand. It has strange-fingered fruit the size of a human hand, its claw-like fingers reaching out from the base of the fruit. It is all pith and no juice. The oils from the fruit and the perfume from the flowers are wonderful.

Splitzer (double-grafted citrus)

The Citrus Splitzer series entered the market a few years ago and was an immediate hit with home gardeners. For people in small spaces who had room for only one citrus tree, the possibility of two-fruits-in-one-tree was enough to fill their hearts with joy. The citrus varieties used for Splitzers are Meyer lemon, Tahitian lime, Navel orange, Japanese Seedless mandarin and Kaffir lime. These are the combinations available:

- Orange and lime
- Lemon and orange
- Lemon and lime
- Kaffir lime and lime
- Mandarin and orange

Double-grafted trees require a bit more maintenance, because you have to keep the two sides balanced. If one side produces much more fruit than the other, prune the most vigorous side. Light pruning can be done all year round, but harder pruning should only take place at the end of summer.

Troubleshooting

Nutrient deficiencies in citrus

Citrus are very heavy feeders and are susceptible to nutrient deficiencies. This will be more noticeable in soils that have either a high or low pH. Testing kits are readily available in nurseries, hardware stores and even supermarkets. Test pH levels in different parts of your garden twice a year.

Soil pH

Gardeners will hear the term 'soil pH' being bandied around by the entire horticultural industry. Soil reaction is measured on a scale known as the pH scale and tells gardeners if their soil is acid or alkaline. Soils with a pH of 0–7 are acid and those with a pH of 7–14 are alkaline. Most plants like to grow in a pH of 6.5 because at this level most of the nutrients in the soil become available to the plant. The pH scale is logarithmic: with every one-point shift in the scale, the number of hydrogen ions changes ten times. So, the difference between a pH of 6 and a pH of 7 may only be one point, but at pH 6 there are ten times more hydrogen ions than there are at pH 7.

The more humus and compost in the soil the better conditions for nutrient availability. In acid soils with a pH of 4–5, nitrogen, phosphorus, potassium, magnesium, calcium, sulfur and trace elements become unavailable to plant roots, causing nutrient deficiencies and interference with healthy plant growth. Soils with a high pH are deficient in iron, phosphorus, manganese, boron, copper and zinc. In soils with a pH greater than 8.5, calcium and magnesium become unavailable.

Raising soil pH in acid soils

Many rural areas around Australia have acid soils, partly due to the type of agricultural fertilisers used over many years. This strongly brings home the point of FEED THE SOIL, NOT THE PLANT for healthy plant growth.

All limestone has some magnesium, which raises the pH in the soil, but the best lime to use is dolomite (calcium carbonate), which can be applied anytime during the year in the following rates:

- Sandy soil: 150 grams per square metre
- Loam: 250 grams per square metre
- Clay: 300–450 grams per square metre

The addition of humus and compost will also help to bring the soil to a more plant-friendly pH level.

Lowering pH in alkaline Soils

Most of Western Australia's coastal strip suffers from highly water-repellent alkaline soils. Again, build up the physical makeup of the soil with lots of humus, manure and compost. Definitely steer clear of poultry manure and use cow or pig instead. One of the most effective elements to lower pH is sulfur. Aluminium and iron sulfate are best in the following quantities:

- Sandy soil: 50 grams per square metre
- Loam: 70 grams per square metre
- Clay: 100 grams per square metre

Nitrogen (N)

Leaves will lose their green lustre and look yellow throughout the tree. Old leaves will drop prematurely and new leaves will be smaller. The tree will experience low fruit set with smaller, inferior fruit. Nitrogen deficiency is more likely in late winter and early spring when the soil is at its coldest and citrus roots go into dormancy. Leaves will turn green again when the soil temperature increases. Nitrogen is needed when plants put on rapid new growth. Nitrogen can be found in animal manures, fish fertilisers, blood and bone and most other fertilisers.

Phosphorus (P)

Phosphorus can be deficient in many Australian soils. The deficiency gives new leaves a bronzed look and makes old leaves look dull and become blue-green to purple (in severe cases). Fruit may be dry and lumpy and the foliage will thin. Apply rock dust with phosphorus, blood and bone with phosphorus, or a complete fertiliser.

Potassium (K)

A deficiency in potassium may cause increased flower fall and fruit fall and irregular brown patches in the leaves during spring. The tips of the leaves will yellow. Apply either sulfate of potash or muriate of potash around the drip line of the tree (see page 32).

Iron (Fe)

An iron deficiency is apparent when the leaves become light green fading to a pale yellow, with the veins remaining green. This is a very common deficiency in alkaline sandy soils and the remedy is to increase the humus and compost in your soil and apply iron chelates to the foliage. Iron chelates will work in the short term only. In the long term you'll have to improve the soil, make an iron compost or increase the amount of clay particles in the soil. You can foliar-spray on spring growth with a solution of 3–5 grams of iron chelates per litre of water.

Handy Hint

To make iron compost mix one cup of iron sulfate to ten litres of moist compost and place handfuls into holes dug around the outer drip line of the tree (see page 32).

Magnesium (Mg)

A magnesium deficiency is seen in the older leaves first. They will yellow from the midrib and blotches will increase until the whole leaf is yellow except a green triangle at the base of the leaf. This happens because magnesium is a constituent of chlorophyll and the plant moves the chlorophyll from the old leaves to the new ones. In severe cases all the leaves will fall. Spread 500 grams of Epsom salts (magnesium sulfate) around the tree and water in well. You could also dissolve 20 grams of magnesium sulfate in 1 litre of water and spray on the foliage.

Manganese (Mn)

Manganese deficiency is more common in very acid soils. If your citrus has a manganese deficiency the younger leaves will have yellow or light-green areas in between the main veins. The veins will remain green but the leaves will eventually go completely yellowish-green. To increase the manganese put 1 gram of manganese sulfate per litre of water in a watering can and pour over the foliage and soil in spring.

Calcium (Ca)

Calcium is needed for cell growth and development. Calcium also helps plant roots access iron, magnesium, potassium and boron. Symptoms of a deficiency are fruit splitting or puffy skin. Adding dolomite lime to acid soils or gypsum to alkaline soils will solve the problem.

Sulfur (S)

Sulfur is an important micronutrient for citrus because it is vital for the process of photosynthesis. It maintains healthy growth across the whole plant. Sulfur will be unavailable to the plant in waterlogged soils. If sulfur is deficient, young leaves will begin to yellow and will grow smaller. The edges of leaves will turn down. You will notice leaf drop and dead twigs developing on the new growth. Fruit will be misshapen, dry and have thick skin. To help the tree, add compost around the drip line and then sprinkle over iron sulfate or gypsum.

Boron (B)

Boron deficiency shows up on the fruit, which will have a typical brown staining just under the skin. The flesh can be dry. The leaves will develop thick veins that can sometimes split and curl under. Leaf colour can be bronze or yellow. Boron is deficient in poor, sandy soils that leach nutrients. Apply an organic fertiliser with boron or apply borax to the soil at the rate of 30 grams per tree and water in well.

Zinc (Zn)

Even though only small amounts of zinc are necessary, it enables a plant to utilise nitrogen and phosphorus where it is most needed. Zinc deficiency will show up in the youngest leaves, with new growth being small, narrow and close together. There will be dappled patches of yellow between the main veins of the leaves and green around the midrib, forming a triangle shape. There can be dieback of small twigs, and new growth will be spindly and weak. The fruit will be much smaller and often elongated. Light sandy soils are usually deficient in zinc. Dissolve 1 gram of zinc sulfate in 1 litre of water and spray on foliage.

Organic pest and disease control

If you go to the trouble of growing your own fruit, it may as well be pesticide free. Citrus are by no means maintenance-free, but there is a safe alternative to most problems. This does not include blokes with chainsaws, who may require more severe measures of containment.

Organic gardeners believe that soil health is directly

related to plant health, and many soil scientists will agree. If your soil is too sandy, too heavy, water-repellent or low in humus, your citrus will be stressed and every insect within a 100-kilometre radius will seek it out for an easy feed.

For every problem listed in this book, an organic or softer solution will be given. For every pest there is a predator, and pesticides kill both. I am thrilled to see the increase in populations of insectivore birds, frogs and beneficial insects – the result of tougher regulations introduced over the past ten years to ban the use of strong pesticides that persist through the food chain. Nature has a plan which includes all players in the game. We should spend more time observing and learning from nature – and less time wanting to kill everything that eats one of our plants.

A word of caution on the softer organic homemade contact sprays: they will also kill beneficial insects. Chilli and garlic, pyrethrum, insecticidal soap, neem and pest oil will kill a ladybird as fast as they kill aphids if it comes into direct contact with the spray. Some fungicides are lethal to bees, so be aware of what else is taking up residence in your garden. Always look before controlling pests.

The importance of birds in the garden

I cannot stress how important it is to create a bird-friendly garden. They are not only a pure delight to watch, but they are the hardest working partners you could ever wish for in your garden. Most birds will put insects on their menu, and some species eat insects exclusively. Wrens and willie wagtails swoop through the understorey catching insects on the wing, or dart around fallen fruit picking off flies. Babblers will flick twigs and leaves over to find hiding insects; swifts and swallows pick off flying insects higher up, and little pardalotes and thornbills happily graze on aphids, scale and lerps that attack your citrus trees. The larger honeyeaters eat all the house spiders that hang around your eaves and pick scale and lerps off your citrus, eucalypts and other native plants. Make birds frequent visitors to your garden and observe them joyfully swallowing up white flies, moths, fruit flies, mosquitoes, grubs and larvae.

The greater the diversity of plants in your garden, the greater the diversity of birds you will attract. Birds have different flight zones and times that they will come and visit. Have plants of varying heights that flower at different times of the year, and always have birdbaths around in a few locations in the garden.

When the NSW Department of Primary Industries did a study of the stomach contents of various insectivore birds, they found that pardalotes had 100 per cent insect content, willie wagtails 69 per cent, and honeyeaters 75 per cent. How wonderful knowing all this is being done without you, the gardener, lifting a finger. All we need to do is provide a garden that offers shelter, a food source and water.

On the topic of building bird-friendly gardens, the manna that grows on eucalypts as a result of sap-sucking insects like psyllids is an important food supplement for birds when nectar is in short supply. I have witnessed honeyeaters and pardalotes feeding on this carbohydrate-rich treat when they have babies in the nest.

If you are serious about having lots of different species of birds in your garden, think like a bird. Look at where a bird might feel safe. Is there protection for them in storms or from excessive heat or cold? Is there a nesting site where babies are safe from predators? Is your birdbath near a large bush or tree so that they can escape if they feel unsafe? If you can provide this and a constant supply of water, you have created a bird haven for our little feathered friends.

Attracting beneficial insects

We need to change our whole perception of the insect world. Gardeners have a habit of classifying them as either good, bad or just plain ugly. It's important to remember that all insects are an integral part of the food chain. If you allow a natural balance to evolve in your garden, regardless of whether they are beneficial to your gardening or not, insects will play a key role in allowing you to become a lazy gardener with nature at your doorstep.

Beneficial insects can now be purchased to release into our gardens, but it is vital to understand their life cycle, the climate they suit and the best release time.

Ladybird and its larva (not to scale)

Predatory insects need:

- A reliable food source
- A safe place to breed
- A safe area to escape from cats, dogs, and other predators
- A reliable water supply

Ladybirds are actual beetles and there are over 400 different species in Australia. They eat aphids, scale and larvae. Ladybird larvae look similar to some pests so pay attention.

Lacewings are the delicate fairies of the insect world. Lacewing larvae, also known as antlions, are less delicate, more rapacious and eat ants, lerp, thrips, scale, whitefly, two-spotted mite and aphid larvae. A lacewing larva can eat up to 400 aphids before growing into a pupa.

Praying mantises are wonderful attackers. With bizarre 180-degrees-swivelling heads, these guys like to eat their prey fresh and wriggling. They devour aphids, flies, adult mantises, caterpillars and grasshoppers.

Predatory mites chow down on the two-spotted mite and bean mite.

Robber flies are large and fierce. They attack the larvae of houseflies.

Hoverflies come into our gardens in large groups and hover around flowers that are rich in nectar and pollen. Their larvae prey on all the sap-suckers, such as aphids, that hang around your citrus blossom.

It may take a few years for a natural balance to establish in your garden, but it is certainly worth the wait. Allow pest insects to exist as a food source for the predators. If it is reliable, they will stay and do all the work for you.

Homemade pesticide sprays

Garlic and chilli spray

In a blender, blend 6 garlic cloves and 4 red chillies. Mix this in 1 litre of cold water and let stand overnight. Sieve to remove large particles, add 3 drops of dishwashing liquid and spray on plants.

White oil spray

Thoroughly mix 2 cups of vegetable oil and $^1/_3$ cup of dishwashing liquid. Dilute 1 tablespoon of this mix in 1 litre of water. This will control mealy bugs, scale and aphids.

Coffee snail killer

Make a strong pot of plunger coffee and dilute 1 cup of coffee with 3 cups of water. Spray on foliage and on soil where snails harbour.

Pure soap spray

Dissolve 225 grams of pure laundry soap in 9 litres of water. Spray on the leaves of your citrus, allow to dry and then hose it down the next day with clean water. This will kill mites, aphids, scale and whiteflies.

Homemade fungicide sprays

Milk, chamomile, bicarb of soda and Condy's crystals have been used for years as preventative sprays for edible crops. I must highlight that they are preventative and do not enter the tree's cellular system. It is good practice to use preventative sprays in humid, wet conditions when fungal spores proliferate.

Milk spray

Use organic full-cream milk that has all the good probiotics. Use the ratio of 1 milk to 10 water. Spray the entire tree including the underside of leaves. Do not make this mixture stronger than 1:10 as you may find it grows sooty mould in humid climates.

Bicarbonate soda spray

Mix together 2 teaspoons of bicarbonate soda, 1 teaspoon of vegetable oil and 2 drops of dishwashing liquid in 1 litre of water. This spray helps to control black spot and powdery mildew because it makes the surface of the leaf too alkaline for fungal spores to grow.

Condy's crystals (potassium permanganate)

Dissolve 1 gram of Condy's crystals in 1 litre of water and spray over all leaf surfaces. Helps control powdery mildew and black spot.

Chamomile tea

Make a strong pot of chamomile tea using the leaves. Cool, strain and spray on foliage for mildew.

Pests in citrus

As with all fruit trees, there will be insects that come and delight in your produce, and weather extremes that give your citrus a bad hair day. Add to this your own compulsion to over-water, over-fertilise and relocate and you may encounter a few setbacks along the way to citrus bliss. Regardless of the problem, you will need to do a bit of detective work before you choose the best solution.

When a tree is stressed it will attract many pests. Sometimes there is more than one problem but they could be related. It is important to understand your pest. You need to know if it sucks, chews, scrapes, burrows, pierces or simply lands briefly. Understanding the mechanisms by which insects feed, breed and develop will help you choose the best time to control them. Get a good magnifying glass to identify pest and predator. If there are natural predators like ladybirds and lacewings, do not spray at all. Leave them to do the work and they will repay you by becoming permanent residents in your garden.

Diseases are a little trickier and by the time you see the symptoms, it's too late for preventative spraying. Early diagnosis is vital to prevent major outbreaks and spread of disease to the whole garden. Products like Ecocarb, made from potassium bicarbonate, are good preventatives and will not harm beneficial insects. If you constantly use broad-spectrum fungicides, you risk killing off the beneficial microscopic fungi that live in the soil. Identify the disease before using a control measure. Other products such as Bactivate, which is packed with beneficial bacteria, work in the soil to destroy bad bacteria and fungi. It's a sort of fire eat fire concept. There are quite a few companies now that are producing beneficial soil microbes to help combat soil-borne diseases.

Below are lists of the most common pest problems found in citrus trees.

The suckers

Aphids

The two aphid species that attack citrus are *Toxoptera aurantii* and *Toxoptera citricida*. They are black, 1–2 mm long and will drive you nuts when citrus gets its lush new growth as they happily suck the juices from buds, leaves and tips. The months from September to October and February to April are the worst. What you do need to know is that they will suck the sap from your tree and breed very quickly as they give birth to live young. Some are winged, others walk from leaf to leaf. They produce a sticky substance known as honeydew, which attracts ants with whom they have a symbiotic relationship. The ants protect aphids from predators and in return are supplied with copious amounts of honeydew. It's like ants going to a free lolly counter. A lovely little arrangement, you might think. However, sooty mould (a fungus) grows on honeydew and reduces a plant's ability to photosynthesise. As aphids are sap-suckers, they also have the ability to spread viruses, like the dreaded tristeza virus. When everything is combined, the tree feels stressed!

An aphid will feed and grow rapidly, outgrowing its skin several times. If you look closely at an aphid infestation with a magnifying glass, you will notice the white papery skins of their former self. Some species of aphids will produce 3–6 young per day depending on the temperature. They don't really like extreme temperatures or heavy rain – these decrease populations dramatically.

Organic control: insecticidal soaps, AzaMax, Eco-Oil, Beat-a-Bug, pyrethrum, garlic and chilli spray, various horticultural oils.

Natural predators: insectivore birds, ladybirds, wasps, hoverflies, lacewings. Grow companion plants, like any daisy flowers, to attract these beneficial insects. I actually still prefer the squishing method that can change the colour of your fingers to a lovely green.

Handy Hint

Remember that natural insecticides will also kill your beneficial insects so only spray once you have checked there are no predatory insects around.

Bronze Orange Bug (*Musgraveia sulciventris*)

This bug is about the same size as the Crusader bug – 25 mm – but has a bronze or black colour, depending on age. These bugs go through five nymph stages with very pretty coats and as many wardrobe changes as a diva – they have a different one for each stage. The damage to the citrus is similar to that inflicted by the crusader bug, with new growth dying off once attacked. They have a foul smell and secrete an offensive liquid as a response to predators. Bronze orange bugs are another Australian native and can be found most of the year, except for extremes of heat or cold.

Organic control: hand-pick using gloves and drop into a bucket of water with 10 ml of eucalyptus oil. Garlic and chilli spray, AzaMax.

Natural predators: insectivore birds, praying mantis, chooks.

Citrus Scale

There are literally hundreds of different species of scale, most of them having a protective coating to shield their eggs from predators. Some scale are host-specific, meaning they will only attack one plant species; others are much less fussy and will go for anything that has sap. Scale are divided into two categories: soft-bodied and hard-bodied. This is not a division between scale that work out at the gym and those that lounge around just drinking sap milkshakes. It refers to the coating that hides the insect beneath. The coatings can be quite ornate and come in many different colours and textures. All scale are sap-suckers, and some even attach themselves to the roots of plants, making control measures difficult. And my, my how they breed. Some species are devoid of males, so the girls are doing it for themselves and reproduce without their assistance. If they get into their stride they will produce between several hundred to several thousand eggs in a lifetime.

Like aphids, scale produce honeydew that the ants farm and help protect. Honeydew allows sooty mould to grow and reduces your tree's ability to photosynthesise – control the pest and you control the sooty mould.

There are many scale that attack citrus and if I listed them all you would probably decide to give citrus a miss. But in fact they don't really pose a threat for the home gardener and are easy to control. They will move around when they are young, but are lazy and hardly move when they reach adulthood.

Organic control: pyrethrum, Nature's Way Insect & Mite Spray, Eco-Oil. PestOil can be used when temperatures are under 32°C, and a second time 3 weeks later to kill the crawlers.

Natural predators: birds, green lacewing larvae, adult and larvae of ladybird, assassin bugs, earwigs, praying mantis, native caterpillars. The parasitic wasp *Aphytis melinus* appears to be successful in controlling scale.

Citrus Whitefly (*Orchamoplatus citri*)

The whitefly is a small white sucking insect that loves the warmer weather and breeds with enthusiasm. The main whitefly that affects citrus is only 2.5 mm long and will hang around on the underside of leaves. Nymphs will secrete honeydew, which will grow sooty mould. Some tips to help your citrus are pruning in the centre of the foliage to improve air movement inside the tree, and hosing down the foliage on very hot days to drop their numbers.

Organic control: PestOil, Eco-Oil, garlic and chilli spray, pyrethrum, AzaMax, Beat-a-Bug.

Natural predators: lacewings, ladybirds, spiders, hoverfly larvae, beetles.

Crusader Bug (*Mictis profana*)

Don't be deceived — the yellow cross on this bug does not mean it is a soldier of righteousness (actually, neither did it during medieval times). But like the crusaders of old, it certainly does smell. Kids call them stink bugs. They are light brown in colour and 2–2.5 cm long. The younger nymphs have only two pale-yellow dots and don't form the cross until they reach full adulthood. They love to suck the sap on the tips of many plants, causing wilting and dieback on the new growth. As they are a native bug, they take up residence in our gardens for most of the year.

Organic control: hand-pick using gloves and drop into a bucket of water with 10 ml of eucalyptus oil. Garlic and chilli spray, AzaMax.

Natural predators: assassin bugs (*Pristhesancus plagipennis)* and small wasps which parasitise the eggs. Some birds, lizards, frogs, bandicoots and chooks will be up for the challenge.

Mealy bugs

These little buggers will attack anything on a plant — roots, stems, leaves and flowers. They will feed on thousands of plants, and especially love those with a high concentration of nitrogen, so beware of over-fertilising. Their numbers will explode very quickly so you will need to control them as soon as you notice them. There are several species of mealy bug that feed on citrus, some with long tails, some with short, but all are soft-bodied and segmented like a slater. They are around

3 mm long, coated in a fluffy white waxy material and will be found under the calyxes of fruit or on leaf buds. Spraying is difficult, as the eggs, live young and insects are underneath the waxy coating. Only spray when crawlers are active. They produce honeydew and so will attract ants and sooty mould. Control the mealy bug and you will eradicate the other problems.

Organic control: Eco-Oil, PestOil, Nature's Way Insect & Mite Spray (check temperature guide if spraying in summer and spray a second time 3 weeks later to kill the crawlers).

Natural predators: birds, green lacewing larvae, adult and larvae of ladybirds, the native beetle *Cryptolaemus montrouzieri*. In addition, parasitic wasps will control mealy bugs by laying their eggs inside the host body.

Mites

All mites are tiny and spider-like with eight legs, love the hot weather and you probably will only be able to see them with a magnifying glass (except for the two-spotted mite). There are a few mites that attack citrus. You will notice where they have been. Do not use miticides as mites build up resistance to these very quickly. The organic control measures detailed below are the same for all species of mites.

Citrus Bud Mite *(Aceria sheldoni)*

If you have citrus bud mite, your fruit will look like aliens have taken over its body. Lemons and oranges will be twisted and contorted with bizarre fingers emerging from the fruit. These mites feed on new flowers and leaf buds, causing the strange distorted shape in the fruit. You may also notice rosetting of leaves at shoot tips.

Organic control: when you notice a swollen bud, pinch it out and either bag it or spray with wettable sulfur, sulfur dust, or Nature's Way Insect & Mite Spray.

Natural predators: ladybirds, green lacewings.

Two-spotted Mite *(Tetranychus urticae)*

These little fellas love the hot weather and will breed up extensively on capeweed. Get rid of the capeweed and you will reduce the population by half. They feed on the underside of leaves, making the leaf tissue spotty. You will notice these little blighters: they have two tiny bright-red dots on their back.

Organic control: when you notice a swollen bud, pinch it out and either bag it or spray with wettable sulfur, sulfur dust, or Nature's Way Insect & Mite Spray.

Natural predators: ladybirds, green lacewings. You can now buy predatory mites that eat the two-spotted mite.

Citrus Rust Mite *(Phyllocoptruta oleivora)*

These are so tiny you would need a microscope to see them. They feed on immature green fruit and cause a mottled brown streaking on it. They harbour on the underside of leaves and only attack fruit that is near the leaves.

Organic control: when you notice a swollen bud, pinch it out and either bag it or spray with wettable sulfur, sulfur dust, or Nature's Way Insect & Mite Spray.

Natural predators: ladybirds, green lacewings.

Passionvine Leaf Hopper (*Scolypopa australis*)

A native insect that is 8 mm long and attacks a large range of plants including grapevines, passionfruit, citrus and other ornamentals. The adult has brown, mottled, transparent wings and looks a little like a moth. The nymphs are pretty wild-looking characters with fluffy white tails that stick up in the air. They look like the punk rockers of the insect world. As the name suggests, they hop or jump along the plant, sucking the sap from new growth and multiplying quickly.

Organic control: pyrethrum, chilli and garlic spray.

Natural predators: all insectivore birds.

Spined Citrus Bug (*Biprorulus bibax*)

A little native bug about 2 cm long that plays on citrus in New South Wales and Queensland and looks very similar to the green vegetable bug, but has fierce horns on its shoulders. The adult bug is green with a shield-like back in a prominent V-shape. The nymphs can be anything from yellow or green to black or orange, depending on their stage of development, and are rounder than adults. The bugs suck both leaves and fruit, causing mottling on the fruit, which goes dry and brown inside.

Organic control: neem oil, insecticidal soap.

Natural predators: birds, parasitic wasps.

Thrips

Hard to see as they are tiny dots on the backs of leaves and are white or pale-yellow when young, turning black when mature and around 2 mm long. If you knock leaves onto a white sheet of paper you will see them. They have a rasping mouth where they lap up the sap, causing a silvery appearance to the leaves of plants. Their numbers drop significantly in very hot or humid weather. Citrus thrips feed under the calyx of developing fruit, which causes a halo around the fruit when it matures. This affects its keeping ability after harvest. You may also notice twisted and deformed leaves and flower parts.

Organic control: pure soap spray, Nature's Way Insect & Mite Spray, PestOil, garlic and chilli spray.

Natural predators: ladybirds, lacewings.

The chewers

Citrus Leaf Miner (*Phyllocnistis citrella*)

Originating in South-East Asia, this is one of the most annoying citrus pests to plague us and is now found in most parts of Australia. They love new growth and are most active in spring and summer. It is a very small, innocent-looking white moth (2–4 mm) with yellow patches and black spots on the wingtips. A party animal, it comes out only at night and gets its thrills by laying eggs in your citrus leaves. The eggs turn into larvae and tunnel through the leaf for 5–6 days, and 3 weeks later they join the nightclub as their parents before them did. Citrus leaves will have silvery trail marks and will be twisted and contorted and often folded up together with the pupae inside. Because the larvae are inside the leaf, it's a difficult pest to control.

Organic control: keep pruning off affected leaves and burning them, or go hunting at night with a torch and a fishnet, and because it's night-time – you could even wear a pair of fishnets while you're catching moths. Refrain from fertilising your citrus in spring and autumn to avoid the soft new shoots that this miner loves. Botanical oils like Eco-Oil and PestOil can be sprayed during growth flushes.

Natural predators: two parasitic wasps – *Ageniaspis citricola* and *Cirrospilus quadristriatus* – and lacewings.

Grasshoppers

There are numerous grasshoppers that attack our gardens, but the ones that plague citrus are the Wingless Grasshopper (*Phaulacridium vittatum*), Giant Grasshopper (*Valanga irregularis*), Plague Locust (*Chortoicetes terminifera*) and Spur-throated Locust (*Austracris guttulosa*). I have seen Plague Locusts strip gardens bare, including the lawn. I have also seen magpies and chickens so full they can barely fly with the weight of a thousand locusts in their stomachs. Up in the tropics of Australia they have grasshoppers you could put a saddle on. They can eat out your whole veggie patch in a couple of hours. Most locusts and grasshoppers hatch in spring and will go through several developmental stages. It is best to try and control them in their first moults. If you have a plague, try prayer because there's not much else that will help.

Organic control: prayer, mosquito netting, neem oil–based products.

Natural predators: chickens, guineafowls, ducks, insectivore birds, lizards, praying mantis.

Lightbrown Apple Moth (*Epiphyas postvittana*)

What are they doing on citrus, I hear you ask. Apple moths extend their palate to include citrus. The caterpillars are a pretty lime-green and will join two leaves together for protection from predators, then happily chew through the leaves and the stem end of fruit. The adult moth is about 2 cm long and grey-brown, usually seen from spring to autumn. You may notice some webbing on the skin of fruit.

Organic control: caterpillar control products like Dipel, Success and pyrethrum.

Natural predators: parasitic wasps such as *Trichogramma* which parasitise eggs, and braconid wasps that predate the caterpillar.

Rats

Yep, they do eat citrus. Surprisingly, rats (*Rattus rattus*) like to eat all the outside skin and leave the fruit. If your tree is near a fence, a roof or next to other trees that are near those things, you will have little chance of doing anything about it.

Organic control: there are currently no organic rat baits on the market but there are ways of putting out baits that prevent pets and native marsupials from getting to them. They are known as bait stations and they're available at all the major hardware stores. Looking on the bright side, I believe rats make great pets. Another thing you can do to keep rats away is tidy up: rats will be attracted to unkempt compost heaps, chicken coops that are not regularly cleaned and fallen fruit left on the ground.

Natural predators: my father's solution to rat-infested roofs was to place two large pythons in the roof space. As kids, it kept us entertained for weeks.

Weevils

Western Australia has had problems with weevils in citrus orchards for some time. The main culprits are Apple Weevil (*Otiorhynchus cribricollis*), Garden Weevil (*Phlyctinus callosus*) and Fuller's Rose Weevil (*Asynonychus cervinus*). Most of the damage is done to the leaves, but the fruit can also be affected.

Organic control: weevils can be trapped by tying corrugated cardboard strips around the base of the trees. They will need to be 15 cm wide. Weevils eat their way around your garden at night and rest in the cardboard during the day. Once a day remove the cardboard and destroy the weevils. For Fuller's Rose Weevils, who are climbers and prefer higher ground in trees, get hold of some dacron (the kind they use to make pillows and doonas) and wrap it around the tree branches like fairy lights. The weevils will get stuck and hopefully make a tasty meal for birds.

Natural predators: insectivore birds.

The piercers

Citrus Gall Wasp (*Bruchophagus fellis*)

The work of these wasps looks like strange growths emerging on the stems, thorns, twigs and veins of leaves. The gall is a reaction of the tree to a tiny black wasp

(3 mm long) that lays its eggs inside living tissue. As the eggs grow into larvae, the gall becomes bigger. Wasps lay eggs in spring and by December the gall will be very noticeable, even to the novice gardener. By autumn you will think your lemon tree is taken over by aliens. The larvae can take up to two years to hatch into adult wasps and the tiny holes in the galls are their exit holes. They usually attack lemons, grapefruits and the finger lime. In severe infestations, citrus trees will have reduced vigour and fruiting. The citrus gall wasp is native to New South Wales and Queensland, which is one good reason to live in Western Australia – they haven't arrived here yet.

Organic control: cut off and burn galls as early as possible to prevent the adult wasp emerging to lay more eggs.

Natural predators: parasitic wasps and ants.

Citrus Nematodes (*Tylenchus semipenetrans*)

Nematodes are microscopic worms that live in the soil and will make your life hell. For such a small worm, it packs a heavy punch and can harbour in all varieties of citrus. This is where rootstock selection comes into play. Trifoliate orange (*Poncirus trifoliata*) rootstocks are highly resistant to citrus nematode and Troyer citrange is moderately tolerant. Citrus nematodes feed on plant tissue from the outside and are termed ectoparasitic (another expression to use at a party). If you had an electron microscope, you would see the little buggers push their hindquarters into the soil, getting into a better position to jab their mouth into the roots. Bit like the rugby scrum position for the big push.

Although this doesn't actually kill the citrus tree, it greatly impairs its ability to pump up water and nutrients from the root system to the whole tree. It will lose vigour, reduce crop and wilt readily in hot weather. The pierced areas of the root system will also be more susceptible to bacteria and fungi attack.

As the nematodes are in the root system and are microscopic, it is difficult to diagnose until you notice the tree is stressed and pale. You could dig around the roots and see if any of them have sticky knobbly bits. These are the egg masses extruded by the female nematodes.

Organic control: the type of nematode will have to be identified, which is a job for your local agriculture department. There are many native nematodes and most of them are good, which is why I would never recommend the stronger pesticides. There is a range of pathogens and predators in the soil, including some fungi, bacteria and other microorganisms, that predate on nematodes. Building up beneficial soil microbes and adding compost will help to keep them in check. If you live in areas where the citrus nematode is found, always use nematode-resistant rootstock (see pages 28–30).

Fruit Fly (*Bactrocera tryoni* and *Ceratitis capitata*)

This topic is as big as big as you can get and usually brings out all the remedies from the Middle Ages that were used to ward off evil spirits and the plague. This is because fruit fly are the world's worst fruit pest and are found in just about every country in the world. Fruit fly don't limit their appetite to just fruit; they will attack vegetables, nuts and ornamentals. They lay their eggs into the fruit, and the larvae cause it to ripen prematurely and rot on the tree. You will be left with a soft weeping sloppy mess full of maggots. In Australia we have over 80 species of fruit fly, but only two major pests – the Queensland fruit fly (Qfly), *Bactrocera tryoni*, and the Mediterranean fruit fly (Medfly), *Ceratitis capitata*. Common to both is their life cycle and the damage they do to fruit.

Fruit fly are very active from mid spring to early winter, but in warmer climates they persist in your garden all year round. The adults will overwinter in sheltered areas, but Medfly will also overwinter as pupae in the soil or fruit. By spring they are out getting to know your stone fruit more intimately. Over recent years there have been cases of fruit fly attacking citrus; if this happens you know that the numbers of fruit fly in your area have built up substantially. Although adult fruit fly only live a few months, they can sure pump out the puppies. One adult can lay up to 1,000 eggs in its short lifetime. Thank heavens insects don't give out a baby bonus!

The eggs hatch within 3–5 days and grow into maggots about 9 mm long. Over the next 3–7 weeks they eat their way through your fruit. If the fruit drops to the ground the maggots will burrow into the soil and pupate ready to start the next generation. The pupation period lasts for 1–7 weeks for the Qfly and 2–7 weeks for the Medfly. Wasting no time for long walks on the beach, within 1 week the adults emerge from the soil and immediately mate, eat and lay eggs. Part of this story may sound familiar to many women. The fruit fly population will build up all spring and summer until the cooler weather hits and they will overwinter to watch the football.

If you have chooks, read this next bit carefully. Although the burrowing habits of fruit fly might sound boring, this bit contains vital information in the control of fruit fly and your chooks can't read. Fruit fly pupation depth will depend on soil type (sandy, loamy, clay) and the moisture content of the soil. If you have dry sandy soil Medfly pupation depth will be about 3 cm. In other soils pupae have been recorded to burrow to a depth of 7.5 cm. If you incorporate your fruit trees into the chook pen, its residents will feast on the Medfly larvae. In dry loose soil Medfly larvae were discovered to emerge from 32 cm. This is clearly too deep for even the biggest chook to forage – you would need something the size of a pterodactyl. Which means other Medfly control measures are also necessary.

Both types of fruit fly need protein and food to mature their eggs. Their favourite menu consists of bird poo, honeydew from aphids and scale, and of course nectar from your stone fruit. The girl flies have an ovipositor that is used to deposit the eggs into the fruit. The Medfly is only 3–5 mm long and light brown in colour. Its only endearing quality is the loveliest pair of mottled brown wings. The abdomen is brown with two light-coloured bands. Western Australia is the only state to be burdened with this pest, and its range is as vast as the state. You may notice the flies around your fruit bowl inside with their little wings outstretched to show how sweet they are. Quite the connoisseur of food, Medfly will attack over 200 species of fruit and vegetable, and even resort to your fruit bowl if the larder is looking low. Unlike the backpacking Qfly, Medfly will tend to hang around your fruit trees where they will carry out all stages of their life cycle.

The Qfly looks more like a wasp and is about 7 mm long with a reddish-brown colour and bright yellow markings. Qfly is native to the humid regions of north-eastern Australia, including the Northern Territory, Queensland and New South Wales. Quite the traveller, it will move through bushland, forest, commercial properties and your backyard. It is known to attack over 60 species of native fruiting trees. If you are lucky enough to live in (or are visiting) areas where fruit fly has not yet struck, you should report any hint of this pest's presence to your state's department of agriculture. These areas are designated Fruit Fly Exclusion Zones and you cannot take fruit or fruiting vegetables into them, by risk of major fines.

Organic control: all fruit tree owners MUST carry out fruit fly control. If you think you will not be able to do this, then don't grow any trees that fruit. Fruit fly is a major problem for commercial growers and government, who spend millions of dollars each year trying to control these pests. Not only that, your neighbours who may be diligent about their fruit fly control will not appreciate your indifference, as your flies will definitely go visit their side of the fence. If you are the one with a slack neighbour, go over and offer to spray and bait their trees when you do yours. Here are the measures you can take:

- **Hygiene:** the most important factor in fruit fly control. Never let infected fruit lie on the ground, and pick and treat any fruit that has been stung. You can either put infected fruit in a black plastic bag, tie a knot at the top and leave it in the sun for 7 days, or put the fruit in a bucket with water and a splash of kerosene for 5 days. Medfly will survive in water for many days so the kerosene is necessary to cut off their supply of oxygen. If you use the plastic bag method you can later feed this to the chooks or livestock, but keep the bag away from crows, rats, dogs and other hungry pests.

- **Pruning:** prune your tree to a manageable size where you can easily spray, bait and pick the fruit. If the fruit is too high up in the tree you will be less likely to spray effectively or pick ripening fruit.

- **Chooks and bantams:** many people incorporate their fruit trees into the chook enclosure. Chooks will scratch up and eat emerging adults, larvae and pupae, and any fallen fruit. Fearless and vigilant, these little home-helpers will also reward you with eggs.

- **Exclusion bags:** these are individual bags you tie around the fruit that give total protection from fruit fly. They are available in different sizes and some are more like a sleeve that fits horizontally off the branch. They are also used on crops such as tomato, capsicum and eggplant. You should use trapping and splash baits in combination with exclusion bags to reduce fruit fly populations.

- **Trapping:** traps are more effective if they are hung in trees all year round to diminish adult populations. They attract the adults using pheromones, aromatic food or visual means. Pheromone traps contain a male or female hormone which attracts the adult, and insecticide inside the trap, which kills the fly. Wet or food traps contain a liquid that has a source of protein attractive to both sexes. The pH of the liquid food appears to be an important factor, as they seem to prefer an alkaline level. A relatively new trap has entered the market called CeraTrap – a bait specifically for capturing Medfly but which is also effective against Qfly, especially females. It is made up of hydrolysed proteins and has been highly successful. If you have a chook pen, you will need to put CeraTrap around it as fruit fly will be attracted to the proteins in chicken manure. Place the traps 5 metres apart at 1.5–2 metres above the ground in a shady part of the tree – this will capture any adults in the area.

- **Homemade traps:** traps need to have several entry holes at the top of a container (such as a plastic bottle) and at least 3 cm of liquid (see recipes). You will also need a cap or cover that protects it from rain. You could put two traps in each tree and one in a non-fruiting tree to lure them away from your fruit trees. The entry holes should have a diameter of 8 mm for Medfly and 10 mm for Qfly.

Trap Recipes

Many people have their own favourite recipes, some containing horse urine, but for the less adventurous try these ones. Your kitchen cupboard seems a lot less risky than running down a horse.

Traps will need to be cleaned and refilled every few weeks. Remember during hot weather the liquid will evaporate and may need filling more often.

Qfly traps
- 1 litre water
- 1 cup sugar
- 1 tablespoon dry yeast
- 1 tablespoon vegemite

Mix all ingredients and place in a jar for 4 days before using.

Medfly traps
- 600 ml water
- Juice of 3 oranges
- 25 grams baking powder
- 1 gram potassium carbonate (potash)

Mix all ingredients and dilute 1:10 with water.

- **Foliage splash baits:** these are sprays that contain a food attractant (protein) and an insecticide such as spinosad (derived from soil bacteria and classified as organic). The female fruit fly needs the protein in order to mature her eggs, but both male and female adult Qfly and Medfly are attracted to the bait. The bait is applied as a thick spray aimed at the middle of the tree on the trunk, stems and centre foliage. Splash baiting should start as soon as you have fruit fly caught in traps, or at least 7 weeks before fruit ripens, or when fruit reaches half-size. Apply the bait in the morning when fruit fly are at their most active. After gorging on the bait, the insecticide kills them. Try not to get bait onto the fruit. In high-risk areas you can apply the bait to non-fruiting trees. You will need to reapply the bait after rain.

- **Cover spraying:** this treatment involves an insecticide spray that completely covers all parts of the tree to kill fruit fly at various stages of its life cycle, from egg to adult. However, this will not prevent the female from stinging the fruit. At the time of printing there was no registered organic cover spray. Organic alternatives to cover spraying include Eco-Naturalure, Nature's Way Fruit Fly Control, CeraTrap and Wild May Fruit Fly Attractant. The bottom line is that no single control measure will protect your trees from fruit fly. You will need to use a combination of traps, splash baits and exclusion bags if you wish to protect your fruit organically. Personally I think it's well worth it.

Diseases in citrus

Citrus are susceptible to a range of diseases in Australia. Coastal areas in the Northern Territory, Queensland and New South Wales with high rainfall and humidity will have higher incidences of fungal diseases like melanose, lemon scab, brown rot, collar rot, sooty blotch, phytophthora root rots and armillaria. If you are in an area of high risk, it is good practice to use protective copper-based sprays before disease sets in.

The drier inland growing regions will have less of a problem with fungal diseases but citrus may still be susceptible to brown rot, collar rot, septoria spot, greasy spot and citrus blast (black pit).

Good citrus management techniques will help reduce the occurrence of disease. Trees should be kept free of dead wood and the canopy kept open with regular pruning. This will allow better sunlight penetration and air circulation, making fungus less likely. Prune off any branches hanging down to the ground to reduce the likelihood of pathogens being carried from the soil into the tree or fruit during rainfall.

The use of copper sprays for citrus

Gardeners will notice many references to the use of copper-based sprays for disease control in citrus. It is useful to know how they work, how they are affected by water quality and the possible damage they may cause.

Copper sprays are more of a preventative and protective fungicide – they are not systemic and are only effective where the spray sticks on that part of the tree. In contact with water, copper solubility increases as the pH drops on the plant's surface and releases a supply of cupric ions. The ions come into contact with the fungal spores or bacteria, pierce through their cell wall and upset their enzyme activity.

In the world of copper sprays there are five basic compounds coming in the form of wettable powders, wettable granules, liquid suspensions and aqueous liquids. They are:

- Copper oxychloride
- Copper hydroxide
- Tribasic copper sulfate
- Copper ammonium
- Cuprous oxide

Copper sprays have better coverage of leaves, and therefore are more effective, if the metallic copper particles are small.

Water quality is critical to the efficacy of copper sprays. If the water pH is too high (7.0) the copper product will be insoluble. As the rate of solubility increases so too does the release of copper ions. On the other hand, a pH of below 6.0 may cause burning, so test your water before mixing up your sprays. The ideal pH for your water is 6.0. If your water is not suitable for use, you can either capture rainwater or buy distilled water.

Copper sprays may cause spotting of leaves and fruit in midsummer, so avoid using them in temperatures above 25°C.

Armillaria Root Rot (*Armillaria luteobubalina*)

If you have this, you're in trouble. The cluster of toadstools that you see in autumn are just the fruiting body of the fungus; the big part, called mycelium, is under the ground and can cover metres. By the time the toadstools emerge it is too late to do anything but remove the infected tree. It is also known as the honey fungus because of the brown coloured mushrooms that emerge at the base of the tree on the outer bark. It lives on woody debris and dead trees. Armillaria spreads by sending its strands of rhizomorphs into the roots of other plants. Threads can also be found between the bark and the inner wood. The tree wilts and leaves turn yellow. The roots will be infected, causing citrus to defoliate, dieback on stems and eventually die. If you peel back the bark, you may see the fine white threads – it's a slow, persistent death.

Organic control: remove any infected plants including stumps and roots and remove soil. Add compost, drench the area with beneficial microscopic soil fungi and bacteria and leave the spot vacant for many years. Soil biostimulants such as Bactivate increase the good microscopic bacteria that can fight fungus.

Black Pit (*Pseudomonas syringae*)

Black pit is a bacteria and appears as light-brown pits in the fruit. You will also see symptoms on the twigs and leaf petioles in the form of reddish-black lesions. This particular bacteria likes cool wet weather and will enter the tree through damaged tissue caused by hail or heavy rainfall.

Organic control: remove all infected fruit and dead wood and destroy. Spray with an organic copper-based spray such as Bordeaux or copper oxychloride in autumn and a follow-up spray 6 weeks later.

Black Spot (*Guignardia citricarpa*)

A problem in the tropical zones that affects the fruit and leaves. Immature fruit will have brown-black speckles on the skin. These become depressed spots up to 1 mm wide and turn either orange or red. In some cases the spots are as large as 3 mm. Once the fungus has reached an advanced stage, the fruit will not be edible.

Organic control: spray with an organic copper-based fungicide with the addition of a horticultural oil to help the fungicide stick to the leaves and fruit.

Brown Rot (*Phytophthora citrophthora*)

There are many species of phytophthora and more are being discovered every year. This soil-borne fungus causes root rot and collar rot and the premature death of many of our native plants. The spores of the fungus move through water and will infect any fruit or branches that come into contact with the soil. Unfortunately snails can also spread the spores into the canopy of citrus trees.

The spores of the soil-borne fungus are spread through water, so when it rains the fungal spores move into your plant. Once infected, the fruit develops a mould and the smell is very distinctive. Brown rot will be seen on the fruit, which becomes bruised and soggy looking. The fruit then falls to the ground and starts the cycle all over again.

Organic control: use an organic copper-based spray, particularly around the times of heavy rainfall and warm weather. Prune off all lower branches where rainfall may splash up and touch the tree. Use biostimulants for the soil and keep adding compost.

Citrus Scab or Lemon Scab
(*Sphaceloma fawcettii* var. *scabiosa*)

A fungal disease that is a serious problem in all lemons, limes, a few mandarins and rough lemon rootstocks. It is more prevalent in coastal areas than dryer regions. As the name suggests, the fruit develops warty lumps and scabs on the skin. These lesions become pinkish-grey or brown as they age. The bark of the tree looks mottled, and yellowing leaves have a spotty appearance. The spores on the scab pustules are spread by wind, water, insects and birds and the spores overwinter on fruit inside the canopy of the tree.

Organic control: only copper sprays such as Bordeaux are currently registered to control scab, but timing is everything. Apply the first spray at quarter to half petal fall, then a second copper spray 4–6 weeks later. The fruit surface is protected from infection by the layer of copper.

Rain will eventually erode this layer so you may need to reapply to protect the spring and summer crops. Burn all diseased material.

Collar Rot (*Phytophthora citrophthora*)

Collar rot is the same nasty soil-borne disease that causes brown rot and root rot. Lemons seem to be most susceptible and the rotting is usually confined to the trunk. It loves wet weather and will travel up the trunk if organic matter or mulch is in contact with the trunk. The first symptoms will be gum oozing out of the trunk near the ground. The leaves will turn yellow and drop off. Then the bark will become wet and eventually dry out, cracking and peeling away from the trunk. If left untreated the fungus can ringbark the tree or travel up the tree causing limbs to die back.

Pop off to the hardware store and get yourself a citrus tree surgical kit. It will consist of a scalpel, a paintbrush, a mixing bowl, a packet of Bordeaux and a white lab coat just for dress-ups. If you have never used a scalpel before, I recommend a packet of bandaids as well.

Collar Rot Repair Kit

Using your scalpel, cut away all the cracking bark from the trunk until you reach the hard wood. Cut all the way to the ground. Go further in until you reach healthy wood.

Now mix up the Bordeaux powder with just enough water to make a thick paste and paint the whole area that you have scraped. Dig a little of the soil away from the trunk and paint this as well.

The most important prevention measure for collar rot is a combination of hygiene and good tree management. Always prune off branches that fall near to the ground when laden with fruit, keep mulch well clear of the trunk and remove any weeds that grow around your tree. Burn all infected bark, leaves and fruit to prevent reinfection.

Grey Mould (*Botrytis cinerea*)

This fungus is not too much to be concerned about but it attacks the flowers and the immature fruit of trees, particularly on lemon trees. Symptoms include grey-green spores on the fruit or blossom. If the flowers become infected, the fungus reduces fruit set and forms ridges on the fruit. The fungus will live on decaying debris, and spores are spread via wind, rain and insects. Grey mould (also referred to as botrytis) prefers damp, wet conditions and cool temperatures.

Organic control: to reduce the incidence of grey mould, apply an organic copper fungicide such as Bordeaux as soon as rain is forecast. Remove all infected fruit.

Melanose (*Diaporthe citri*)

In coastal and tropical regions of Australia this is one of the most important diseases that cause downgrading of fruit. It is more common in older citrus, particularly lemons and grapefruit. Dead wood that is left on the tree or fallen branches left on the ground allow the fungus to survive. The spores are released during rainfall and splash up onto the fruit. Warm humid wet weather allows for spore germination that will eventually penetrate the fruit or stems.

The early symptoms appear on fruit, leaves and twigs as small brown-black spots that are slightly raised. Fruit looks like it has fly poo all over it or, when the disease is more advanced, tear-stains. Rain carries the spores down and along the fruit. If citrus trees are under stress due to drought or poor drainage, melanose will attack the leaves and stems. The bark will produce brown stains with streaks of yellow gum oozing from the bark. Leaves will have dirty red-brown spots and will eventually yellow.

Organic control: remove all dead wood to reduce the inoculum load of the fungus and burn it, keeping it well away from the tree. All fallen leaves should also be removed. Copper-based sprays are effective at controlling melanose, but timing is critical. Copper forms a protective coating over fruit, making it hard for spores to penetrate the skin. Bordeaux can be applied to the fruit at half petal fall and again 4–6 weeks later. Copper is more of a protectant and will not kill off the fungus that already exists in the dead twigs and stems. Diseased material must be removed. Prune out the centre of the tree to increase sunlight and air circulation to the canopy to discourage fungal spores.

Penicillium – Blue Mould (*Penicillium italicum*) and Green Mould (*Penicillium digitatum*)

If you have a neglected fruit bowl that only gets cleaned out every fortnight, you would definitely have been growing some penicillium on your lemons or oranges. The fungi will invade the smallest hole, nick or tear in the skin cells and grow rapidly. Once the mycelium has entered the cells, the spores spread in a circular pattern and make the fruit seem water-soaked. Penicillium is a contact mould and spreads to other fruit that it touches. It has a pungent smell – you will notice it as soon as you get near the fruit bowl. The same mould that you see in your fruit bowl can grow on the fruit in your tree.

Organic control: good hygiene and management around citrus trees. Remove any fallen fruit and do not touch a healthy fruit after handling an infected one. At home, clean out your fruit bowl more regularly or drink more lemon juice.

Septoria Spot (*Septoria citri*)

Septoria spot used to be a major problem for growers who used overhead irrigation. Rain splash would carry the spores onto the fruit from leaf litter, infected twigs and dead wood. The rind of infected fruit displays brown sunken spots of up to 16 mm. Sometimes the spots meet up to form a sunken brown crater with a reddish rim.

Septoria is most active in autumn and prefers damp cool weather with extended rainfall.

Organic control: spray citrus trees with an organic copper-based spray like Bordeaux or copper oxychloride at the end of March or just before the autumn rains.

Sooty Mould (*Capnodium* spp.)

The presence of sooty mould indicates that you have honeydew-excreting insects like aphids and scale on your tree. The mould grows on these sweet sticky secretions and is basically a superficial fungal mould that grows on every part of the tree. It doesn't actually penetrate the fruit, stems or leaves, but reduces the tree's ability to photosynthesise. Honeydew is manufactured by aphids, scale and mealy bugs (see the pest section of this book), so control the insects and you will eliminate the sooty mould.

Organic control: spray a horticultural oil, Nature's Way Insect & Mite Spray, Beat-a-Bug or pyrethrum to drop the sap-sucking population. Then get a laundry bucket, put in half a cup of Lux flakes and dissolve in warm water. Hurl the contents over the tree, leave it for a few hours and blast off with the garden hose. This will help shift the remaining sap-suckers and break the mould off the leaves and branches.

Stem-end Rot (*Diaporthe citri*)

This is a spore-producing fungus that deposits itself on the fruit in wet conditions. It will remain dormant until the fruit begins to ripen, then appear as a light grey-brown circular patch at the end of the fruit. Small branches may also die back as the fungus spreads throughout the tree.

Organic control: remove and destroy all fruit and infected twigs and branches. Spray tree in autumn with an organic copper-based spray like Bordeaux.

Environmental or non-pathological problems

Dry granulated flesh

This is when the individual cells in the fruit are dry. It can be caused by drought, a boron deficiency or sap-sucking insects that attack the fruit when it is young. There are a few solutions to this: you can spray an insecticide for the sap-suckers, pray to [insert appropriate deity here] for rain or apply a solution of boron at the rate of 4 grams borax to 4.5 litres water and pour around the soil. This will treat up to 5 square metres.

Frost burn

Frost burn causes browning of the leaves and eventual leaf drop. Remove all mulch from under the tree during frost season as it holds in the cold around the root system. Some gardeners completely wrap their trees in shade cloth, but if you have a large tree this can be difficult. If you are really worried, get one of those small kerosene lamps and safely place two under the outer canopy. Apparently this works for many plants – looks quite pretty as well I would say. You could have a little winter solstice garden party and invite any wandering druids in for a drop of red.

Citrus growers go weak at the knees if frosts persist as they can lose their whole orchard. In all seriousness, it is important *not* to prune any frost-damaged growth until the risk of frost is over. If the trunk or branches have been burnt by frost, they will be susceptible to sunburn that summer, so paint the affected areas with a water-based acrylic paint.

Fruit drop

Nearly all citrus will drop fruit because it bears too many flowers. Only around 9 per cent of flowers will produce fruit, which is still a substantial number. Do not be alarmed when you see the majority of the tiny fruitlets drop off the tree. Some mandarins, oranges and kumquats are biennial, so fruit more one year than the next. On the big crop year, make sure you give them adequate fertiliser and water to cope with big production. The most common reasons for fruit drop are tree stress or splitting fruit. Gardeners who live in very hot, dry areas will also notice fruit drop when temperatures rise above 34°C, especially after hot winds.

Good management of trees is no cure for weather extremes, but foliar feeding with liquid seaweed and fish or crustacean-based fertilisers may help trees hold their fruit.

Fruit splitting

Fruit splitting is more often noticed in autumn when temperature and rainfall fluctuate and is more common on young trees. Navel oranges are the most susceptible, but some mandarins and tangelos will also split. There can be many causes and it will probably be a combination of them: temperature fluctuations, moisture stress, irregular fertilising, lack of calcium or copper and sudden heavy rainfall.

Handy Hint

Large puffy green fruit with thickened rinds is caused by too much nitrogen and not enough phosphorus.

Green oranges

If you live in tropical Australia, you will be used to seeing green oranges and grapefruit that are fully ripe. Valencias have a habit of almost turning orange before turning once again to green. Nothing to worry about, but if you want them to go orange or yellow, put the picked fruit in a paper bag with a banana or a couple of ripe apples and the ethylene gas these give off will change the colour.

Leaf drop

Severe spikes in temperature (either frost or heat), water stress, nutrient deficiencies, waterlogging, and root restriction can all cause excessive leaf drop. I guess for the home gardener, it's a process of elimination. It can also be caused by an overexcited gardener who sees flowers appear and gets a bit heavy-handed with the fertiliser. This is very common. Citrus leaves should remain intact on your tree for a few years, and then drop. Strangely, if your citrus drops all its leaves, it has a habit of going into full flower just so you don't rip it out. Needless to say if you let all of the new flowers fully fruit it will cause some stress and you may have to nurture it back to health over a couple of years. The better approach is to remove half of the fruit when it's marble-sized.

Salt burn

Often related to over-fertilising, salt-laden winds or salty bore water. The edges of the leaves will be brown and dry and branches may turn black and die back. If you live right on the coast you will need to hose down the foliage on all your plants once a fortnight or create a salt-tolerant wind barrier as a front-line defence.

Sunburn

All parts of citrus trees can sunburn on extremely hot days (above 42°C). Never prune your citrus severely before the hot summer months as exposed trunk and branches will burn. Apply a white acrylic paint if you think this may happen. Remove any fruit that has dull soft skin. If you know you are in for a killer summer, put up a shade shelter for a couple of months, particularly when trees are young.

Thick skins

Unlike humans, as some citrus trees get older they develop a thicker skin. If you have a tree that grows puffy dry tasteless fruit with a thick skin, pull it out and have another crack at growing citrus. It's related to either age or poor environmental conditions, so put your energy into a new tree. One of the major causes in younger trees is too much nitrogen. Little and often, folks, little and often.

Extra bits

Recommended reading

Birdscaping Australian gardens: A guide to native plants and the garden birds they attract, George Adams (2011). Vaucluse, NSW: D&G Publishing.

Citrus: A guide to organic management, propagation, pruning, pest control and harvesting, Allen Gilbert (2007). Flemington, Vic: Hyland House Publishing.

Citrus for everyone, Bruce Morphett and Ian S. Tolley (1999). Adelaide: Botanic Gardens of Adelaide.

Organic fruit growing, Annette McFarlane (2011). Pymble, NSW: ABC Books.

The complete book of fruit growing in Australia, Louis Glowinski (2008). Sydney: Lothian.

The Garden Guardians, Jane Davenport (2006). Byron Bay, NSW: Imaginality Pty Ltd.

Organic information: handy websites

Sustainable Gardening Australia	www.sgaonline.org.au
Green Harvest	www.greenharvest.com.au
Organic Crop Protectants	www.ocp.com.au
Eco Organic Garden	www.ecoorganicgarden.com.au
Fly Bye Fruit Fly Lure	www.nutri-tech.com.au
AgriSense Fruit Fly traps and lures	www.entosol.com.au

Departments of primary industries by state

New South Wales	www.dpi.nsw.gov.au
Northern Territory	www.nt.gov.au/d/primary_industry
Queensland	www.dpi.qld.gov.au
QLD Fruit Fly Hotline	1300 135 559
South Australia	www.pir.sa.gov.au
SA Fruit Fly Hotline	1300 666 010
Tasmania	www.dpiw.tas.gov.au
Victoria	www.dpi.vic.gov.au
Western Australia	www.agric.wa.gov.au

Acknowledgements

I would like to thank all the keen gardeners and writers in Australia who constantly share their knowledge with others so that we can make better choices, help green the planet, feed ourselves more sustainably and have heaps of fun in our gardens.

My children Jessie, Tom and Lucy for giving me the excuse to change my gardens to suit their various life stages.

Finally to the wonderful people at Fremantle Press who encouraged me and supported me with great humour and patience as I completed this book.

cheers!

About Sabrina

Sabrina comes from a long line of obsessive gardeners and decided to make a full-time career out of mucking about in the garden. She started landscaping at the age of four, stripping flowers and foliage from her grandmother's garden and creating fabulous miniature gardens in all her Nan's baking trays. This she found to be excellent grounding for garden design work later in life. At the age of twenty-two she found cake tins to be a bit limiting and decided to study horticulture more formally at Bentley TAFE. During this time she started her own landscaping business in Perth, specialising in Australian and Mediterranean-style informal gardens. Her passion still remains with creating gardens that reflect the diversity of nature and encourage us to interact with the natural environment in a caretaker role.

Sabrina fell into her radio career at the ABC in Kalgoorlie in 1985 and has worked in ABC gardening talkback radio ever since. Few media presenters last that long but Sabrina's lively character and unorthodox manner of delivering gardening stories have kept her listeners enthralled: she makes gardening fun.

Sabrina's work in remote Aboriginal communities in Western Australia's Kimberley region has been a huge success. She has helped to set up many edible gardens in the communities and has worked closely with women elders to grow bush tucker plants so that traditional knowledge of their use can be passed on to the next

generations. Sabrina also guides overseas cultural tours for Australians Studying Abroad and loves travel.

Sabrina's main achievement in the industry is sharing her love of gardening and vivacious zest for life with the listening audience so that they learn, through gardening, the important role nature plays in people's lives.

A-Z Index

M